The Battle

Clive Corfield

New Wine Press

New Wine Press
PO Box 17
Chichester
West Sussex PO20 6YB
England

Unless otherwise stated, all Scripture quotations are taken from the
HOLY BIBLE, NEW INTERNATIONAL VERSION. Copyright © 1973, 1984
by International Bible Society. Used by permission.

NKJ – New King James version, copyright © 1983 by Thomas Nelson,
Inc.

ISBN 1 874367 90 6

Typeset by CRB Associates, Reepham, Norfolk
Printed in England by Clays Ltd, St Ives plc.

Acknowledgements

Every stream has many tributaries and the stream of my life and ministry is no exception. Indeed the contents of this book is a mixture of personal revelation, experience and the input of many who the Lord has used to formulate my views and mould my philosophy of ministry. I would therefore like to acknowledge the many that have contributed to this work and supported me down through the years.

My mother and father who have always been there even when I confused and worried them terribly.

Chris and Jan Mungeam who stayed by me when everyone else fled.

Jean and Elmer Darnall who taught with patience and took risks with us so we could learn and grow.

Bob Gordon who inspired my heart and challenged me to walk by faith.

Graham Powell, who probably saved my life with his teaching, support and ministry.

Peter Horrobin who trusted me to teach and taught me so much about the healing ministry.

Marc Dupont who releases the life and presence of God and enables me to see things more clearly and keep things in perspective.

Steve Hepden, my mate who is loved by so many and is always such an encouragement. We continue to stand together (whenever possible!)

John and Carol Arnott who believed in me and loved me to wholeness and helped me to live again.

Doug Williams who down through the years has always been a friend and wise counsellor.

Alan and Doreen Hodson who labour with us in the work of Sovereign Ministries making things happen in their right order and at the right time. For typing and correcting this manuscript. Again!

Pat, Janet, Johnathan, John, Wendy, Jean and the rest of the Sovereign Ministries team (you know who you are), who have stood together in many places in many countries ministering the love and power of Jesus into countless numbers of people down through the years. Who have also covered my back when exposed and prayed until the breakthroughs came.

For the pastors who have taken the risk and opened the doors of their churches and by God's grace saw the hand of God at work in people's lives.

Mel and Jeanette the best outlaws who continue to support and be involved in every way.

Thank you.

Dedication

Karen, my precious wife, who came into my life like a breath of fresh air and who now stands with me in every respect a partner, friend and lover.

Laura, Sarah, Benjamin, Joshua, Kathryn, my children and my friends through whom I have learned so much about the Father's heart.

Thank you.

Contents

Foreword

During the last several years I have been asked to review and/ or write endorsements for many books. Mostly they are good, sometimes they are very good, but once in a while they are vital. It is with pleasure that I write this foreword as I believe this book to be in the vital category.

Despite possible differences in eschatological views, it is obvious to most Christians today who have any global awareness of what God has been doing the last 20 years or so, that God, in our lifetime, is doing incredible things. In fact, we are at least partially, seeing the 'knowledge of the Glory of God covering the world as the waters cover the seas.' But that means more than just the Church increasing numerically. It also speaks of the beautifying of the Church as we learn to respond to the Bridegroom – Jesus Christ!

Clive, along with his wife Karen, have powerful insight and wisdom in understanding the working of the Holy Spirit in helping the Church move closer towards being living reflections of His Glory. I have known Clive and Karen well for almost a decade. We have ministered together extensively in a variety of church and conference settings in two different continents. I also count Clive as one of my closest friends. I have not only personally heard and seen Clive minister in much love, power and wisdom, but I have also been the recipient of blessings from God through Clive.

The reason I feel so strongly about Clive and this book, is that in the years of our close friendship I have seen Clive live out exactly what he is speaking of. Perhaps this is something that sets *The Battle* apart from many other books available in the same genre. Clive has lived through deep disappointments and times of almost overwhelming frustration in life. He has gone through intense times of testing. I have spent times with Clive and Karen when we have prayed, laughed and wept together. But consistently, they have kept loving and serving the Lord Jesus and the Body of Christ. Clive has, in fact, lived through the dark night of the soul, but he has not taken his eyes and heart off the Lord. The result is that Clive has 'taken the head off his giant', as described in chapter 5.

Clive has, not only theoretically but experientially as well, become an overcomer. He has realized the victory through Christ. The fruit of his faithfulness is a man who has much to offer the Body of Christ in the knowledge of walking with God even through the valley of death.

Clive also has a deep prophetic side to him in understanding the times and seasons of what the Holy Spirit is doing. *The Battle* is extremely timely, as it is time that we Christians move on from just having a message, to being the message.

I highly recommend this book to all, and I pray that God uses it as a powerful tool of encouragement in your life to help you realize the fullness of what God the Father created you for.

Marc Dupont
Mantle of Praise Ministries
Ft. Wayne, Indiana, USA

Preface

I have written this book seeking to encourage and strengthen the floundering, challenge the complacent and stir the hearts of those who love the truth of God's word and want to live it out in their lives.

I am sure you will identify with most of the stories I share because they are real and honest. I also trust that the teaching will produce fruit that will last. Unfortunately I have met so many who have been gifted, called and anointed but have fallen to sin or become so discouraged they have given up. This has been mainly due to a lack of foundational discipleship or the absence of healing and deliverance in their lives from the effects of their background. Regrettably many have ended up a victim to their own selfish desires, or are taken out by the enemy because they do not know how to defend themselves.

I hope this book expresses the passion I have to see the Body of Christ rise up in power and authority, living in victory even in the midst of adversity. I trust too that it will inspire you not to settle for just having a theology of victory, but making biblical truth a reality in our lives.

I long to see Christians confronting the things that resist us, realising that we will never know victory unless we engage in battle. Joshua looked over the Promised Land and was assured by the promise of God that it was his for the taking, but he had to go in and possess what was rightfully his. Like Joshua, we too must take back from the hand of the enemy what he has stolen from us, and enter in to all that God has provided for us through the cross.

I hope this book will in some way help you to move forward in faith and power.

Clive Corfield
Lancaster
May 1999

Chapter 1

You Will Never Know Victory Until You Have Been in a Battle

'But thanks be to God! He gives us the victory through our Lord Jesus Christ.'　　　　　　　　　　　(1 Corinthians 15:57)

A sobering reality check

Many of us who know and love the Lord Jesus may frequently declare that we are more than conquerors through Christ who loved us. Countless songs have been written and sung about the victory of the Church over the world. Indeed the Church rightly believes it has victory through the power of the cross, but all too often the sad reality is that our churches are full of defeated, broken people who are being overwhelmed, infiltrated and polluted by the world. Where is the reality of victory? The tragic situation is that the divorce rate in the church is similar to that outside the church, and there is as much sickness in the church as there is outside of it. Christians are in as much debt as unbelievers are and many of us who profess Christ appear even less happy and fulfilled than those we seek to witness to!

There is a challenge that comes to us all when asked the question: 'what is the difference between us and non-believers in the way we live our lives?'

Acts 1:8 tells us that we *'shall receive power when the Holy Spirit comes upon us and we shall be witnesses ... '* To enable us to witness to the reality of the resurrected Christ we need more than theology or new church structures and programmes. These are very helpful, but are in themselves inadequate. What we need is the power of God! And this power needs to be applied into our lives for it to be of any effect; otherwise we will only have the theology of victory, but an experience of defeat.

We may seek to offer an impression which says we are more than conquerors, yet continue to live with our fear, rejection, unconquerable sin, compulsive behaviour patterns, lustful thoughts, greed, arrogance, pride and every other kind of damage and sinful condition known to man. This inevitably renders the Church weak and ineffective against the onslaught of evil. It is clearly by the grace of God alone that the Church stands today, for we read in scripture that Jesus said He would build His Church and the gates of hell would not prevail against it. **My desire is to encourage us to take our theology and turn it into a reality of victory within our lives**, so that we, the Church, really can stand strong in Christ.

If we are honest most of us avoid the opportunity and bypass the right to possess our possessions in Christ. Instead we have a tendency to wait for someone to wave a kind of spiritual 'magic wand' over us so that victory can come to us as an automatic consequence of our actions. This often takes the guise of asking every visiting evangelist to pray for us, or needing to receive a word from the passing prophet. Evangelists and prophets are essential to the body of Christ and their input is vital as they express their role in building up the body to equip the saints for works of ministry. The mistake is made when we expect them to do everything for us and depend upon them to give us a quick fix of blessing rather than seeking the face of God for ourselves.

The Bible tells us that Joshua had to go in and possess the land that God had already given to him (Joshua 1:6). The theme of the Lord giving the enemy into His people's hands is repeatedly demonstrated in other scriptures. **It is a fact that the battle had to be fought to realise what had already been secured in the spiritual realm through God's promise.**

One of the problems we face is that we live in a very 'instant' age: instant entertainment, instant food, instant education have to some degree rendered our generation lacking in the ability to 'dig deep' when necessary, and we now find it an alien concept to fight and work for what is rightfully ours.

I expect, like me, you may have discovered that when we press into what is rightfully ours or begin to uproot the enemy from his place of occupation he often offers a token resistance! It is at this point we may tend to give in rather than press on to take hold of the victory which Jesus won for us at the cross.

The lesson of Pickles the cat

Years ago our family owned a cat called Pickles who was an odd looking animal with major personality defects. We had taken her in as a stray but she never really got over early traumas in her life! Some evenings she would climb onto my lap and curl up in a ball purring quietly. However, when I tried to move from my position she would instantly dig her claws into my leg, seeking to hold me down in order to remain comfortable. At this point I was faced with a decision – did I spend the rest of my life with a cat on my lap, or should I stand up and shake her off? Obviously I stood up and the cat jumped to the floor twitching her tail and looking most indignant. This is so often the way it is in our lives when we seek to make a move forward to progress in Christ, or to move the enemy from his occupation. He then begins to offer resistance and it's at this point we have a choice to make. Do we spend the rest of our lives accommodating spiritual immaturity and demonic oppression, or do we lay claim to our rights to be free in Christ, shaking the enemy off by the power of the blood of Jesus and the authority in His name?

Effort – the scary word that might bring change

While it is possible to maintain a belief of victory, we may have no real intention of engaging in a battle to obtain what is rightfully ours in Christ. The truth is, however; **we will never know victory until we have been in a battle**. So often we want our victory served on a plate through the laying on of hands or fulfilling a certain formula. The truth of the matter is that spiritual maturity, development and growth does not come through these things, but through surviving the many unavoidable battles of life.

> *'Praise be to the God and father of our Lord Jesus Christ, who* **has** *blessed us in the heavenly realms with* **every** *spiritual blessing in Christ.'* (Ephesians 1:3)

Here God reveals to us that we have already been blessed with every spiritual blessing in Christ Jesus. This is truth. It is the word of God, it is His promise to us all who are Christians, but the reality is that we rarely see the fulfilment of this truth and promise because we fail to act upon it in faith.

> *'. . . faith by itself, if it is not accompanied by action, is dead.'* (James 2:17)

There will be some effort needed on our part to take hold of that for which Christ has taken hold of us. It is difficult to respect those who live in continual defeat, accepting the bullying and buffeting from the hand of the enemy without making any attempt to change their circumstances. With the help and power of God, which is available to all who know and love Him, we can succeed.

It is only when we have lived through the reality of a war and emerged on the other side, perhaps carrying a few dents in our armour, slightly blood-stained, bruised and scarred, that we can stand with some dignity and say 'In Christ I am more than a conqueror. I have fought a good fight.' There has to be a reality of overcoming in our lives!

We can be sure that the enemy recognises the true level of

our authority in Christ; whether it is superficial and theoretical or experiential, practised and forming a deep and intrinsic part of our lives.

God's promise to us is true, and if we will only give Him room to work in our lives and trust Him enough to see us through the battles, we will achieve our heart's desire.

> *'I waited patiently for the LORD; he turned to me and heard my cry. He lifted me out of the slimy pit, out of the mud and mire; he set my feet on a rock and gave me a firm place to stand. He put a new song in my mouth, a hymn of praise to our God. Many will see and fear and put their trust in the LORD.'* (Psalm 40:1–3)

Ziglag – an unlikely place of blessing

In 1 Samuel 30 and 31. we read the amazing story of King David during one of the most stressful and difficult times of his life. David and his men had been in exile from their own people and land. They had forged allegiance with the Philistines who had just rejected them and would not allow them to form part of their army. David's men returned dejected to Ziglag (the town which had become their home) to discover that an Amalekite raiding party had been going through the country stealing and destroying as they went. This was made easy because the Philistine fighting men had all gone off to war. David and his men had started off with them, but were now returning home rejected. When they arrived at Ziglag, they found to their horror that their town had been burned by fire by the Amalekite raiding party who had also carried off their wives, sons and daughters.

David and his men wept aloud together at the loss until they had no more strength to weep. Then the men's grief turned to anger as the reality of the dreadful situation began to dawn on them and they even began to talk of stoning David because they were so bitter in spirit. It is at this point we can see the true character of David beginning to emerge.

Instead of running, or slipping into a slough of despond he threw himself back upon the Lord.

'But David found strength in the Lord his God.'

(1 Samuel 30:6)

When we are met with awful circumstances it is easy to become bitter and be overwhelmed with grief and pain. While it is natural and correct to express pain in a rightful way, we need to throw ourselves back upon the Lord to see how He may want to resolve our situation. If we do not turn to Him we can become locked into the circumstances and never move on from the pain and grief.

It is such a blessing to see how God can turn adversity around into tremendous victory if we are willing not to give up too soon and go God's way instead.

Submerged in the past

Dr Martin Lloyd Jones told the story of a bed-ridden man he was asked to visit. Upon his arrival the man began to tell him the tale of his traumatic experience during the war years. He told how his submarine had been damaged by a depth charge and shared in graphic detail the horror of the events of that fateful time. He described the terror as they were plunged into darkness as the lights went out following a tremendous explosion. He talked of the fear as the water flooded the vessel and how the screams of his fellow sailors fell silent as they hit the bottom of the ocean.

The visiting minister asked him to finish the story, but the bed-ridden man just repeated the same tale word for word, finishing with 'and it all went silent as we hit the bottom of the ocean.' Dr Martin Lloyd Jones again asked him to finish the story, but the bed-ridden man just kept repeating the same horrific incident finishing with 'and it all went silent as we hit the bottom of the ocean.' 'Will you not finish the story?' asked Dr Jones. The man replied 'What else is there to say? It was horrible, we just sank and it all went silent as we hit the bottom of the ocean.' 'Well,' declared

Dr Jones 'you're not at the bottom of the ocean now are you?' and continued 'at some point someone must have rescued you to enable you to lie in your bed today to relay this horrible incident. You are no longer at the bottom of the ocean! You have been saved! You are alive!'

Unfortunately, many people are locked into the horror and failure of their past, frozen in time, unable to see the good that came out of the bad. While I am not diminishing the trauma, pain or horror of such incidents, the Father will heal these areas of our past if we let Him in. However, it is vital in the process of healing and recovery that we, like David, strengthen ourselves in the Lord our God and seek His face to see how we can best respond for Him to turn the circumstances around. If we don't, we could get stuck in the past and fail to move on into all the Lord has for us and others whom the Lord chooses to touch through us.

Faith to obey

After David had enquired of the Lord he received a clear word to pursue the enemy. This word from God gave them all faith.

> *'So then faith comes by hearing, and hearing by the word of God.'* (Romans 10:17 NKJ)

How important it is to respond to God's voice. His word is the only thing that can produce living faith within our hearts. Once we know we have heard Him we can respond in obedience and confidence. When we have no idea what is on the heart or in the mind of God we live in presumption or fear, operating in the flesh and not in the anointing of the Holy Spirit.

Prophetic relevance is vital to success in our warfare. Presumption brings death, whereas hearing the voice of God and responding brings life and power.

> *'There is a way that seems right to a man but in the end it leads to death.'* (Proverbs 16:25)

The word from God to David and his men was to pursue the enemy with a sure promise of victory. In response to this, David and his six hundred men set off in hot pursuit, but it was not too long before fatigue set in and two hundred of them felt they were far too exhausted to continue. David left them to look after their supplies and continued with the remaining four hundred men. They eventually caught up with the Amalekites and fought them from dusk until evening of the next day.

This was no easy pushover. David and his men were really going on faith in God's promise because everything in the natural was against them. Out-numbered and overtired they still pressed on to take back that which was rightfully theirs. This battle lasted over twenty-four hours, and was no quick-fix situation. It took faith and tenacity in the midst of fatigue and isolation to achieve what they did.

Motivation

Many of us may well have given up after the initial struggle. I believe however there was real motivation in David's men's hearts because what they were fighting for was of real value to them. They loved their families and counted them worth fighting for, even dying for if necessary. The problem with us can be that we really don't value what the Lord offers us and we therefore allow the enemy to rob us of God's best. We may settle for the 'just enough' and 'this will do', or 'I cannot expect more'. If, however, we truly valued what Christ died for on the cross, we would fight all the harder to see what is of value to Him be realised in our lives. All too often we give up because we really don't appreciate what we are fighting for.

> *'The thief comes only to steal and kill and destroy; I have come that they may have life, and have it to the full.'*
>
> (John 10:10)

Like the Amalekites, the enemy invades our lives and robs us of joy, health, finance, good relationships and so much more. Jesus promised us abundant life, but there are times we have to be willing to fight for it.

That which has already been secured for us by right in the spiritual realm has to be realised in the natural if it is going to become a reality.

Restitution

David and his men overcame the Amalekites and recovered everything they had stolen, with nothing missing. The ironical thing about this story is that the enemy had not only robbed David and his men at Ziglag but this same raiding party had also been stealing from the Philistines. Therefore when David defeated the Amalekites, he was not only able to retrieve that which was rightfully his, but also the whole plunder the Amalekites had taken from the Philistines.

The enemy may have robbed us but Jesus promised us abundant life!

> *'I will give you the treasures of darkness, riches stored in secret places, so that you may know that I am the Lord, the God of Israel, who summons you by name.'* (Isaiah 45:3)

Here I believe God promises us that the treasures of darkness (that which the enemy has control of, stored away in places unknown to us), will be released to us by God's power so that we may know that He is the Lord, the true God of His people.

The Bible also tells us in Exodus 22 that if a thief is caught he must make restitution – he must pay back double what he has stolen. Regarding extortion, Leviticus 6 instructs that the thief must pay back in full, plus 20%.

Jesus said that the enemy is a thief who comes to steal, kill and destroy. Therefore, according to God's word, the enemy must pay back and make restitution. Remember Isaiah 45:3, *'I will give you the treasures of darkness, riches stored in secret places . . . '*?

In addition to this, Jesus promised that He had come to give us abundant life! **Now is the time for us to take back**

from the hand of the enemy what he has stolen from us – with interest!

Maybe this is the reason that James could say in James 1:2–4:

> *'Consider it pure joy, my brothers, whenever you face trials of many kinds, because you know that the testing of your faith develops perseverance. Perseverance must finish its work so that you may be mature and complete, not lacking anything.'*

Perhaps he knew the reality that the enemy would have to pay back more than he stole or destroyed, while recognising that during the process of battle and recovery, the Lord would be doing a deep work in his own life, and that in the end he would be mature, complete and lacking nothing.

Think of what the enemy has robbed from you. What has he destroyed that is precious to you – health, finance, peace, joy, opportunity? Is it worth fighting for? If it is then seek the face of God and inquire of Him how best to proceed.

Sometimes we have to let things go and allow God to restore them to us in different ways to what we expect. Other times He will want us to pursue and take back that which is rightfully ours. He will show us how this is to be done bearing in mind that the weapons of our warfare are not of this world but are powerful to the pulling down of strong-holds.

Either way it will take faith, courage and effort to let it go, yet expect the Father's blessing to return in other ways, or alternatively to pursue and take back from the enemy what he has stolen from you.

However, never lose sight that the Father wants to bless us abundantly but we have to go His way to realise the best.

Chapter 2

What We Have Victory Over

The term 'victory' is often used in Christian terminology so it is worth looking at what the Bible says we have victory over in Christ Jesus.

Victory over death

The Bible teaches us in 1 Corinthians 15 that we have victory over death.

On a gravestone in Scotland is this inscription:

'Remember friends as you pass by
As you are now, so once was I,
As I am now, so you must be.
Therefore prepare to follow me.'

The stark reality is that every one of us is going to die. Death is an unavoidable appointment for every human born into this world, and yet it is the most avoided issue, even within Christian circles. We live our lives as though it were never going to happen to us. Understandably, for those outside Christ, death strikes fear to the very core of their being, even if they do not believe the Bible and its warnings of judgement, and the prospect of having to face eternity without God while experiencing the punishing fires of hell. The alternative atheistic belief in annihilation is not a very pleasant prospect either! However, for the believer in Christ, there is no need to fear, for we are assured of eternal life with Jesus Christ.

'... We will not all sleep, but we will be changed – in a flash ... the trumpet will sound, the dead will be raised imperishable, and we will be changed for the perishable must clothe itself with the imperishable, and the mortal with the immortality.' (1 Corinthians 15:51–53)

Every believer wants to go to heaven, but nobody wants to die. Yet to enter into this glorious new life, and to experience the resurrection from the dead, we must first die. Jesus gave us a definite promise – we would not perish, but have eternal life if we believed in Him (John 3:16). We are assured in John 14 that He has gone to prepare a place for us, and where He is we shall be also, that He alone is the way, the truth and the life, and that no one can come to God the Father except through Him. The Bible also tells us in Revelation 21 that there will be a new heaven and a new earth; the first earth will pass away and there will be a holy city, a new Jerusalem, coming down out of heaven from God, prepared as a bride beautifully dressed for her husband. The dwelling of God will be with men, they will be His people and He Himself will be with them and be their God. Every tear will be wiped away and there will be no more death or mourning or crying or pain. The old order of things will pass away and God will make everything new. What a glorious hope for the believer in Jesus Christ – living with Him in our resurrected bodies, imperishable, holy, radiating the glory of God!

I remember hearing the story of an open-air meeting conducted by the Salvation Army in which there was a procession from their citadel down to the market square. In this procession they carried a coffin, shoulder high, followed by a band that played a dirge. When they reached the market place they laid the coffin on the ground and all gathered around in solemn silence. Onlookers, out of curiosity, gathered around to see what they were all looking at. To their amazement the lid flew open and out jumped General Booth crying, 'Where O death is your victory, Where O grave is your sting?'

This is the victory that Jesus has won for us on the cross. Our sin is forgiven, and the blood of Jesus and the indwelling of the Holy Spirit seal us into a new covenant relationship with God, so that when our bodies die, the immaterial part of us (the soul), goes directly into the presence of the Lord Jesus. As Paul said in Philippians 1:21–24,

> *'For to me, to live is Christ and to die is gain. If I am to go on living in the body, this will mean fruitful labour for me. Yet what shall I choose? I do not know! I am torn between the two: I desire to depart and be with Christ, which is better by far; but it is more necessary for you that I remain in the body.'*

What a living faith! What an expectation! These are the promises of God for us to believe and grasp hold of so that we can shed the fear of death that so grips the heart of the world. For those of us in Christ, death is but a veil through which to pass into a new dimension of life with Jesus.

In this present life we see the things of God in quite an obscure way. 1 Corinthians 13:12 says,

> *'Now we see but a poor reflection as in a mirror; then we shall see face to face. Now I know in part; then I shall know fully, even as I am known.'*

What a joy to see Jesus face to face and to see the heavenly realm as it is in all its glory and splendour. We will experience an environment without pain or sorrow, gaze upon the angelic host and know the closeness and embrace of our saviour and Lord. It is beyond our imagination to know fully what lies in store for those of us who believe, but we do know that we will experience His love and power in its fullness and enter into His purity and holiness as never before. There will be work to do in heaven as well as worshipping Him, and we will be ruling and reigning with Him forever and ever.

Grieving

For most of us the fact that we dread death is not so much based in what lies before us but rather that we fear the means of death, and the sadness of leaving behind those we love and cherish. It is bad enough saying goodbye to my family when I have to leave for a ministry trip for a couple of weeks. How much more painful to leave loved ones for what may be a very long time until we meet again in heaven. There is therefore a realistic sense of loss, grief and pain which all of us experience when we lose loved ones. This, coupled with feelings of loneliness, abandonment, regret and anger, can make death a wretched time even for Christians. However we do have a word from God:

> *'Brothers, we do not want you to be ignorant about those who fall asleep, or to grieve like the rest of men, who have no hope.'* (1 Thessalonians 4:13)

By God's grace we are a people who have hope, and although we naturally grieve we are not like those who have no hope of eternal life with Jesus. The truth is that in our loss and grief we have a sure hope that we will be united again with our loved ones who know and love the Lord Jesus. It may seem a long time until we meet them again, but in fact our life here on earth is a very small period of time compared with eternity. And every believer in Christ has eternity within their hearts.

The means of death

The means of death is another concern. To be faced with the atrocious terminal conditions that take so many would be daunting for even the bravest believer. Even with modern medical facilities the suffering some endure before their demise is immense. Friends of mine who work with the terminally ill have shared with me that often when a person who knows Christ as Lord and saviour and is at peace within themselves, can slip away into the loving arms of Jesus with joy, peace and a sense of victory at their departure. Paul's confession that he *'had a desire to depart and be with Christ, which is better by far'* (Philippians 1:23) seems an appropriate desire for one tired of the battle and wanting to go home to be with their Lord.

This is quite a contrast to those who are outside of Christ with no hope. They wrestle and fight against the inevitable, full of fear and dread, and there is an intuitive realisation in everyone that death holds something awful for them.

> *'Just as man is destined to die once, and after that to face judgement.* (Hebrews 9:27)

God's word is true – all they have to face is death and judgement. What a terrifying thought.

I have at times wondered how those who have had to suffer martyrdom managed to endure such a thing. I can only imagine that God in His mercy gives grace and supernatural strength and courage to see through the hatred, violence and suffering.

> *'Let us fix our eyes on Jesus, the author and perfecter of our faith, who for the joy set before him endured the cross, scorning its shame, and sat down at the right hand of the throne of God.'* (Hebrews 12:2)

Jesus on the cross must have kept His eyes on the Father, trusting Him through the hateful experience to bring Him back to Himself. He would have been focusing not so much on the moment but on eternity.

In a similar way I believe God will give grace in our difficult circumstances to enable us to fix our eyes on Jesus, the author and perfecter of our faith. This was surely true for Stephen in Acts 7, when he claimed to see Jesus and the glory of God at the moment of his martyrdom. Amazing! The truth is that for us in the West this is quite an alien concept, but our brothers and sister in Christ in other places around the world have to face persecution. In fact, there probably has not been a time in the last two thousand years when some have not been required to lay down their lives for the cause of the gospel. A sobering thought, but it somehow puts our often-petty problems into a more realistic perspective.

The unknown

There is also a real and natural sense of apprehension of the unknown. When we travel to a distant land, never having been there before, the experience can be intimidating. We are unsure of what we will find when we get there, coupled with a sense of how far away we are from what is familiar. So it is with death – we have never done this before, it is unfamiliar territory, and we have heard little about it, but are sure it is there.

My Bible College Principal, Elmer Darnall, shared with a few of us once how he was looking forward to dying! He felt it was an adventure that would only pass him by once. Therefore he warned us students that should he die during one of his lectures, no-one was to raise him from the dead, as he was sure he would be far happier with the Lord than with us lot! A couple of years ago I was invited to join in a theological discussion on eschatology. One well-known and renowned speaker attempted to unravel the mystery of heaven asking 'is heaven a state to be in or an actual place?' After his paper, the floor was open for discussion. The more the discussion continued with varying opinions and arguments the more bored I became with the whole proceedings and when given the opportunity I suggested that maybe the promise of Jesus that He had gone to prepare a place for us is true and that we were not to get ourselves into a state!

Jesus did promise us that He was going to prepare a place for us. It is being made ready for each of us personally by Him. What we do know about our resting-place with Him is that according to 1 Corinthians 2:9–10:

> *' "No eye has seen, no ear has heard, no mind has conceived what God has prepared for those who love him" – but God has revealed it to us by his Spirit . . . '*

It might be worth taking time to ask the Holy Spirit to reveal in our hearts something of eternity to give us courage, faith and hope for the future.

Victory in life

The Bible tells us that while we live on this earth we can be more than conquerors through Christ and that we have the potential to live victorious Christian lives. However, there are three common enemies of the Christian, which seek to lock us into death and defeat – the world, the flesh and the devil. Let us look at each of these.

The world

> '*Do not love the world or anything in the world. If anyone loves the world the love of the Father is not in him.*'
>
> (1 John 2:15)

We understand from Scripture that this world is controlled by the devil through demonic powers, which in turn operate through man's sinful nature. When Jesus was tempted by the devil in the wilderness (Luke 4:1–13), one of the temptations offered was that if He bowed down and worshipped the devil He would be given all the kingdoms of the earth. Note, first of all, that Jesus did not contest the fact that they were the devil's to give. Through the deception, disobedience and rebellion of Adam and Eve the devil now had the right to rule the world and influence its values and standards. Whereas originally Adam and Eve would have ruled under God in love, righteousness and justice, now man rules, controlled by evil forces.

Jesus however, made it very clear that the kingdoms of the earth were the devil's to give, because of man's sin, thus giving him rights to operate through man. He made it clear that He had come to take them from him. Colossians 2:15 clearly tells us that Jesus triumphed over all the works of darkness through the cross.

In its present condition, the world reflects little of the Kingdom of God as it did before the fall of mankind. The world's influences put great pressure on Christians to conform to its sinful standards and values. We may often feel humiliated or embarrassed as we stand for the truth of God's word in such a corrupt society. The world mocks at the values of God and in unbelief diminishes His truth. It can be very tempting for us to compromise the high calling of God upon our lives by drawing the world's value systems into ourselves and our churches. However, we are called to influence the world with the values of the Kingdom and to shine as lights in a dark and broken world; not to be polluted by their values, which are in essence demonic. 1 John 2:16 tells us that,

> '... the cravings of sinful man, the lust of his eyes and the boasting of what he has and does – comes not from the Father but from the world. The world and its desires pass away, but the man who does the will of God lives for ever.'

In order to overcome the world and its pressures we must learn to resist temptation and practise saying 'No' to its enticements. We must learn to stand firm on what we know to be true and holy, even when this brings ridicule, mocking and persecution. The Christian is called to live as a light in the world (Luke 5:14). If we do not learn to say 'No' and resist the pressures of the world, we will be forever over-whelmed and impregnated with its values. This will lead us to judge things by our own moral standard, rather than viewing sin from God's perspective. We can see this happening in the Church where there is confusion over clear biblical issues such as sexual morality, homosexuality, honesty, integrity, marriage etc. Additionally we take on the values of the world which do not reflect the Kingdom of God: for example our love of money, personal ambition, the types of music we listen to, the television programmes we watch and the literature we read, some of which we know intuitively Jesus would not be part of, or indeed would be highly offended by.

> 'The eye is the lamp of the body. If the eye is good, your whole body is full of light. But if the eyes are bad, your whole body will be full of darkness...'   (Matthew 6:22–23)

The eyes and ears are gateways to the soul. What enters our mind through the eyes and ears either brings light or darkness. It will build up and edify or will pollute with the values of the world.

Often our conscience becomes less acute and sensitive the more we impregnate our mind with such dangerous things. Let me give an illustration. I believe the devil is seeking to desensitise the population to God's warnings of danger. Many who once would have been horrified at what is transmitted across our television screens now find themselves comfortable with it. What once would have shocked no longer appears to. Horror, occult, perversion, morbid fascination with death, suspense, all these things and more we find commonplace. We have become insensitive to it, even to the point that what we once found revolting has now become a means of entertainment. We watch bodies being tortured and mutilated, rape, sexual perversion, occult promotion; we listen to foul language and something inside is intrigued and drawn towards it in subtle fascination. It is easy to give place to it without realising what we are doing.

However, although we know we are not of the world, we still have to live in it. I have been amused over the years how the church has sought to be holy. More often than not it attempts to put on external appearances that look right, or at least don't conform to what is viewed as being worldly. When I was with one particular Christian organisation we were encouraged not to conform to the world and its ways. This of course was highly commendable, but the way in which they imposed their understanding of holiness was not to be in fashion with the rest of youth. So we all looked odd with our outdated clothes which, together with our listening to non-worldly music, more often than not caused us some embarrassment. Now the truth of the matter was that we were in fashion, only ten years behind everyone else. All clothes were in fashion at some time and we were taught not to conform with the world, which we did, only ten years behind our contemporaries. This is not true holiness, just religious nonsense. True holiness is an issue of the heart, which will express itself in our lifestyle. We can be contemporary and still be holy and unworldly. We can be in step with our peers yet not conform to the sin pressures around. The key question to ask ourselves is 'What would Jesus do?' and then do what you know He would do, watch what He would watch, listen to what He would listen to and turn off what you know to be suspect. Don't give the devil a foothold, stay clean and unpolluted and sensitive to the Holy Spirit, who will lead us into all truth.

> *'Do not be deceived: God cannot be mocked. A man reaps what he sows.'* (Galatians 6:7)

We will reap the fruit of what we have sown into our lives through our activities and associations. Jesus said *'judge them by their fruit.'* Do we display the fruit of holiness or the fruit of worldliness?

The flesh

The second area that bombards our lives to cause defeat and failure in our walk with the Lord is the area of our flesh (Galatians 5:16–32 and Colossians 3:5–10). Here we have the battle from within the soul, the appeal of the unregenerate fallen nature, which seeks to draw us away from righteousness.

Often, when teaching on this subject, I ask for a show of hands in response to the question, 'Who here enjoys sin?' More often than not the people know they are being led into a trap so there is some hesitancy, with a few hands half-raised and others firmly gripping their seats, knowing full well that as good Christians they should never enjoy sin. However, as I explain to them, if sin did not bring pleasure or appeal to something within us then we would never be tempted into it. The very fact that we are tempted means that there is something inside us that desires to sin and indulge in its pleasures. This part of us is, of course, our fallen nature. Today, generally speaking, sin is regarded as outdated and, in many people's view, irrelevant. Nowadays we have 'problems', 'weaknesses' and 'demons'. Of course each of these issues is real and needs to be attended to, but all too often we can hide behind these things and use them as an excuse to evade personal responsibility for our sinful behaviour. More often than not we tend to judge our sin according to our own moral standard, rather than viewing it from God's holy perspective. It is only when we see our lives and the things we engage in from God's perspective that we can receive the gift of repentance and turn away from such acts in the strength of the Holy Spirit.

We are repeatedly told in the New Testament to put off the old man and put on the new. In response to this requirement from God, we need to ask Him to show us our sin and enable us to repent of sin issues in our lives. Repentance means that we turn around, walk away from them and change our minds. There are a number of things that I would still probably enjoy doing today that I enjoyed doing before I came to Christ. They brought much pleasure and a temporal satisfaction. However, when I recognised them as sin and chose of my own free will to repent and turn from them it brought cleansing through the blood of Jesus and renewal by the Holy Spirit. Repentance does not mean that we have to stop wanting to do something, it means that we just stop doing it and God will give us the strength we need. However, when we choose to repent of things that offend God, we can by His grace begin to see just how God feels about sin and know His revulsion ourselves.

Repentance is a choice we make to turn away from sin. It is inadequate just to feel sorry and remorseful for what we know to be wrong in God's eyes or, more accurately, what we have been found out about. When I first began pastoring, a man arrived on my doorstep in floods of tears. He was a pastor in a neighbouring town. I brought him into our lounge and he began to tell of his ordeal. His wife had left him for another woman to engage in a lesbian relationship, his children were in rebellion, his church was dwindling in numbers and he felt wretched and bewildered about his circumstances. He confessed to being domineering and inflexible to those close to him.

However, after much crying we began to talk and it became apparent that in his view everyone had let him down, others were rebellious and they should have loved him as he was. He was remorseful and full of regret and confessed that he wished it all could have been different, but he never expressed his own need of repentance. He was sad yet self-righteous, seeing the sin in others but expecting others to overlook his, even though he knew he was hard to live with. However, his view was that as he was in leadership of the family and of the church, it was the rebellion of others that had given the devil this foothold and brought his life to ruin. He never once wanted to change himself nor did he see the damage he had caused in their lives, although he expected those around to accommodate his controlling and damaging ways unconditionally. There is a saying that 'there is none so blind as those who will not see'. Maybe we need to ask the Father to give us the gift of repentance, to show us our sin and to help us turn from it.

Repentance is only a means to an end and not an end in itself. The desire in the Father's heart is always to bring us to wholeness and healing so that we can fulfil His purposes for our lives. Repentance is part of that process. It brings cleansing and releases us into God's grace and mercy. The devil desires to hold us in self-justification so that we lose out on God's best for us. We are not to wallow around in self-condemnation and wretchedness but allow repentance to be a springboard into abundant life.

The demonic

The other common enemy of the human soul is the demonic.

The apostle Paul wrote,

> '... in order that Satan might not outwit us. For we are not unaware of his schemes.'   (2 Corinthians 2:11)

There was undoubtedly a burden in Paul's heart to communicate to his friends in Corinth that they were not to be unaware of the devil's schemes, otherwise he would outwit them and they would suffer the consequences. It is amazing to me that Jesus spent so much of His time teaching and ministering deliverance openly for all to see, yet the church has, by and large ignored it, even though the subject is so clearly laid out in scripture. This has resulted in a struggling, overwhelmed, ineffective church. In many places Jesus commanded us to preach the gospel, heal the sick and cast out demons, but the church has generally chosen to overlook the reality of the powers of darkness and remain ignorant of the devil's schemes. As a result we suffer the consequences.

C.S. Lewis says in *The Screwtape Letters*:

> 'There are two equal and opposite errors into which our race can fall about devils. One is to disbelieve in their existence. The other is to believe and feel an excessive and unhealthy interest in them. They themselves are equally pleased by both errors and hail the materialist or a magician with the same delight.'

There needs to be a balance in our approach to this subject for obvious reasons. We have probably all come across those who find a demon under every bush and blame the devil for everything that could ever go wrong. Their health, success or achievements for God do not seem to out-strip the rest of the church, which doesn't share their enthusiasm for demon-hunting. Yet there is without doubt a need to acknowledge the reality of the demonic and understand how the enemy works if we are to gain control over circumstances which have caused us to live in defeat, pain and bewilderment.

First of all we must acknowledge that Jesus Christ is the Lord of heaven and earth and that there is nothing in all creation that is not subject to His authority and dominion (Ephesians 1:18–23; Philippians 2:9–11; Colossians 1:15–18). We have a big God and a small devil. God is omnipotent, while the devil is limited in his power and authority. God is omnipresent, while the devil can only be in one place at any one time. God is omniscient but the devil is limited in knowledge. We are told in scripture that the demons scream in terror at the name of Jesus. He alone is the Lord of heaven and earth and all that is in them.

From time to time we all experience resistance to our progress in Christ and our efforts for the kingdom of God. We can identify with Paul when he says that,

> *'Our struggle is not against flesh and blood, but against the rulers, against the authorities, against the powers of this dark*

> *world and against spiritual forces of evil in the heavenly
> realms.'*   (Ephesians 6:12)

Our enemies are not so much those people around us, but
rather the invisible forces operating around, in and through
them. We cannot see these enemy agents with the human
eye but the effects of their existence are felt on a regular basis.
Many sicknesses, adversities, curses, accidents, squabbles and
irrational behaviour can have their root in the demonic.

We see clearly in scripture how Jesus not only recognised
the demonic operating in human lives, but dealt with it
accordingly with the full power of the kingdom of God. In
Luke 4:31 we read that Jesus, while teaching the people on
the Sabbath day, was disturbed by a man crying out at the
top of his voice. Jesus instantly commanded the demon
within the man to be quiet and to come out of him. We
note in scripture that the demon threw the man to the floor,
nonetheless the demon left him without injury. The people
were amazed and wondered where Jesus got His authority
and power from because they had not seen anything like this
before. Again we see in Matthew 9:32 the crowds were
amazed when Jesus drove out a demon that had rendered
a man incapable of speech and instantly the deaf and dumb
man spoke. What we see here is a miracle of healing following deliverance.

I remember ministering in Hungary with friends and we
were preaching the gospel in a small village close to the
Romanian border. The presence of the Lord was there to heal
the sick. During the course of the meeting a mother and
friend brought a young twelve-year-old lad to the front of the
church to receive ministry as he was deaf and dumb and had
been so from birth. Many people had prayed but there
had been no breakthroughs to date. As the young lad came
forward I saw upon him a generational curse of death which I
rebuked in the name of Jesus and commanded to leave him.
The Holy Spirit also showed me that there was a deaf and
dumb spirit upon him which I told to go in the name of
Jesus. At this point the Holy Spirit said to me 'Command

healing in My name.' So I put my hands over the boy's ears and commanded healing to take place in the name of Jesus. When I lifted my hands from his ears he was looking utterly amazed. I asked the translator whether the lad could hear me and he indicated that he could. We then asked him in Hungarian to say 'Jesus Christ is Lord' and for the first time in his life noise came out of his mouth similar to that which we were saying. The boy had received his hearing and his ability to speak because Jesus had healed him after the demonic had been dealt with.

We see again how sickness can be brought about by the demonic with the healing of the woman who had been crippled for 18 years. We read in Luke 13 that this dear soul had been bent double and could not straighten up at all. When Jesus saw her He called her forward and said 'Woman you are set free from your infirmity,' then He put His hands upon her and immediately she straightened up and praised God. What is interesting to note is that two things are at play here – first of all, Jesus declared that she was free from her spirit of infirmity, then after the infirmity had gone He placed His hands on her and healed her.

The Gospels are packed with instances of Jesus setting people free from the power of the demonic. We see in the book of Acts the apostles setting people free from the powers of darkness in the name of Jesus. This, of course, is because healing and deliverance is part of the great commission. We read in Matthew 28:18–20 that all authority in heaven and earth has been given to Jesus, and then He commands us to go into all the nations making disciples and teaching them to obey everything He has commanded. We observe in scripture Jesus Himself ministering healing and deliverance, preaching the kingdom of God, and commissioning His twelve disciples to do the same. We read too that He also commissioned the 70, who came back rejoicing that even the demons were subject to them in the name of Jesus. Now we have the great commission where Jesus is instructing the disciples to teach us everything that He had commanded them to do. In other words we, in making disciples, are also to teach them how to preach the kingdom of God, heal the sick and deliver people from the demonic. We note too in Mark 16:15–20 that Jesus commands us to go into all the world and preach the good news to all creation and that this would be confirmed with signs following. We read in verse 17 that one of the signs would be the ability to drive out demons in Jesus' name.

So we find ourselves in modern-day church seeking to fulfil the great commission! In part we preach the good news of the kingdom of God but we often fail to embrace the full gospel of healing the sick and delivering people of the demonic. Maybe this is something we need to repent of and begin to embrace so that we can see God's people being set free and rising up in victory, instead of living in defeat in so many areas of their lives.

The question which then arises is 'How do we set people free from the demonic in the name of Jesus?' Firstly, we have to look at how the enemy entered his place of residence in our lives. We note that the enemy has a legal right to be anywhere there is sin. Jude 6 tells us,

> *'The angels who did not keep their positions of authority but abandoned their own home, these He has kept in darkness bound in everlasting chains for judgement on the great day.'*

We see here that the enemy, Satan and his fallen angels, when they were thrown out of heaven by Michael the archangel (Revelation 12:7–9), lost their place of authority. However, they still maintained their power or ability, but had no realm in which to operate. They were, in fact, thrown out of heaven down to earth, where they entered the physical realm which we can see, and have been locked into the realm of darkness bound with everlasting chains, awaiting the judgement day. It is this realm of darkness which the enemy is limited to, and in this realm he has a sphere of influence or authority whereby he can exercise his power and ability. This darkness is not so much the absence of light but the realm of moral darkness, a place where God has chosen to absent Himself.

We know that wherever there is sin there is darkness. Jesus, however, came into this world as the light of the world and in Him was no darkness at all. In other words there was no moral darkness or sin within the heart of Jesus, and therefore the enemy had no claims on Him or power over Him. Jesus came from heaven with the full authority and power of the kingdom of God. He came as a light into the darkness because this whole world is polluted with the darkness of the enemy. Jesus penetrated the darkness with the light of His life and His message of the kingdom of God. That is why Jesus' first words in the Gospel of Mark are,

> *'The time is come, the kingdom of God is near, repent and believe the good news.'* (Mark 1:15)

This was His announcement that the kingdom of God was at hand and in order to experience the light and life of this kingdom we need to repent or turn away from the darkness in our lives and believe the good news of salvation.

The first step to being set free from the powers of darkness is to repent of sin so that we might obtain forgiveness for our sins and cleansing through the blood of Jesus (1 John 1:9). This, in effect, robs the enemy of his right to rule and occupy our lives. Our sin is like a stronghold for the enemy to inhabit. When we repent of sin and receive God's forgiveness the stronghold of the enemy is torn down and he is exposed.

Of course one of the characteristics of the enemy is to hide. Back in the late '70s I worked on a missionary ship, and once when I was in the galley celebrating the Chinese New Year with my Chinese friends the main generator failed plunging us all into darkness. It took a couple of minutes for the standby generator to come into action and when the lights came back on the whole of the galley was seething with cockroaches. However, as soon as the light came on, the cockroaches scurried away into every nook and cranny seeking to hide from the light and inhabit the dark, damp, dirty places.

This is illustrative of the way the demonic operates within

our lives. The enemy hates humility, honesty, grace, forgiveness and mercy. He loathes it when those in bondage begin to resist him by going the way of the cross and drawing near to the Father and His grace, because this exposes his hiding place.

One of the significant signs of revival is people coming under the conviction of sin and seeking earnestly to repent and go God's way instead of the way of the world, the flesh or the devil. In simple terms the way in which we can rob the enemy of his place of occupation in our lives is to come under the Lordship of Jesus Christ and allow Him to be God in every area of our lives, our mind, our will, our emotions, our bodies, our time, our relationships, our sexuality. When we truly make Jesus Lord we can repent not only of known sin in our life, but also those sins we have inherited from our forebears.

The next stage in robbing the enemy of his rights of occupation is to forgive all those who have offended us or done us wrong. Jesus clearly told us that we need to forgive from the heart and if we do not forgive then He cannot forgive us our sins. This is sometimes a very hard thing to do when we have been deeply damaged by people and we want vengeance, desiring that those who have offended us be punished for what they have done. However, the gospel tells us that we need to forgive if we are to be forgiven – the devil hates forgiveness and wants to fuel our lives with bitterness and resentment, but this is the 'cancer of the human soul'.

The devil will lie to us and tell us that if we forgive these people we are in effect saying that what they have done to us is unimportant and we are letting them off the hook. However, he will also fuel the pain in our lives which these people have caused, because of our unforgiveness. We must come to the Father and ask for grace to forgive, in order to release these people from our judgement instead of cursing them with our desire for vengeance and vindication. We can choose to bless them which breaks strongholds of the enemy within our lives. God wants to heal the pain which has been caused, but He cannot reach in and heal our hearts if we still allow resentment to fester deep within. We need to make a choice to forgive and allow God to heal our emotions that are so wounded by what has happened to us.

It was grace which enabled Jesus to say on the cross 'Father, forgive them, because they don't know what they are doing.' In the same way we need to ask the Father for grace to say 'Father forgive them for they were operating out of their damage and pain and wickedness of heart; forgive them for they didn't know what they were doing.'

Once we have robbed the enemy of his rights of occupation within our lives, we can then apply the weapons of deliverance to set the captives free. These weapons are:

1. **The name of Jesus** (Acts 3:12–16; Philippians 2:3–11; Ephesians 1:20, 21; Mark 16)

    I have already mentioned that the demons scream in terror at the name of Jesus, so when we pray in His name and command the enemy to go, it is impossible for them to resist Him and His authority. The name of Jesus is not a catch-phrase which we put on at the end of a prayer like a superstition, it is a command with His authority, realising that we are ministering with the full resources of the kingdom of God behind us.

2. **The blood of Jesus**

    'They [that is us] *overcame him* [the devil] *by the blood of the Lamb and the word of their testimony.'*

    (Revelation 12:11)

They did not love their lives so much as to shrink from death. We can overcome the enemy by applying the blood of Jesus specifically into situations.

In the Old Testament the blood of the lamb, which was used for ceremonial cleansing, was applied by hyssop, pouring or sprinkling. From the moment the blood was applied to priests, utensils or buildings, the site of its application became wholly consecrated and set apart for God's use. The blood remaining in the lamb was of no use, the blood remaining in the bowl was of no use, and

41

it was only powerful when it was applied. Now we are in new covenant relationship which the blood of Jesus has sealed us into. We can apply this blood, not by pouring or sprinkling, but by words of faith as we testify to what the blood of Jesus has accomplished.

Apply the blood through confession:

'Through the blood of Jesus all my sins are forgiven, through the blood of Jesus I am a new creature in Christ, through the blood of Jesus the enemy has no power over me or claims against me, therefore I command you to go. The blood speaks of freedom, the blood speaks of cleansing, and the blood speaks of life. Enemy you must go now in Jesus' name.'

3. **Faith**

   These words have to be applied in faith. In Mark 11:20–26 we read that we can speak to mountains and they will obey us. It is possible, therefore, that we can speak to mountains of demonic oppression within a person's life and, if we believe in our heart and do not doubt, that mountain must go.

4. **The gifts of the Spirit** (1 Corinthians 12:4–11)

   When we minister healing and deliverance we must operate in the gifts of the Holy Spirit, receive revelation and know the anointing of the Holy Spirit in our ministry.

5. **The word of God** (Hebrews 4:12, 13; Proverbs 4:20–23)

   We know the word of God is active and powerful; it is like a two-edged sword and the enemy cannot resist the authority of God's word. Often I have given spiritual prescriptions just as a doctor would give medicine to a sick patient. This involves asking them to read a scripture three times a day. I invite them to read it once to God and thank Him for it, once to the devil and rebuke him with it and once to themselves and believe and act upon it. I have found that when a person gets the word of God into their life and starts allowing it to be lived out through them, the enemy is significantly weakened and deliverance is so much easier to minister.

Ministry dynamics

One thing I have noticed over the years is that volume does not equal authority! It is unnecessary to shout at the demonic to get a response, even deaf spirits recognise the authority of Jesus operating in and through you! Remember at all times that we are ministering to people who are loved by God and are precious in His sight, therefore maintain dignity and show sensitivity to them.

It is, of course, possible for us to set ourselves free from the enemy's works. We can rebuke the enemy in our own lives and tell him to go. We must keep praying and commanding until he does leave.

Once a person has been set free from the demonic, it is essential that they are filled with the Holy Spirit and that they close the enemy's entrance into their own lives by living in righteousness. Otherwise, as scripture teaches us, the enemy will seek to return, and, finding the place clean and unoccupied he will enter again, but this time with seven of his friends. To avoid this happening we need to ensure that we encourage those to whom we are ministering not to revert to the sins which were the doorways for the demonic in their lives. They must continue to resist the devil so that he might flee from them and draw near to God so that He might draw near to them.

Chapter 3

Living in Victory
in the Midst of Adversity

Adverse circumstances

We can so often become overwhelmed by problems and circumstances that seem beyond our control. We can find ourselves locked in a struggling marriage or in a job we hate, confined to a wheelchair or bedridden, isolated from other adult company, trapped in the home as a single parent, unemployed without any prospects, or any one of a whole host of other stressful situations.

Unfortunately, due to adverse circumstances in our lives that produce enormous frustration, we often feel anger and resentment as a result, creating a bubbling cauldron of emotion inside. Additionally, through deep disappointments and a feeling of no escape we may begin to sink into despair. It is at this point we view life through very negative eyes and often with an overwhelming sense of hopelessness. Our anger, which is often directed at other people (normally those whom we love and are close to) is probably anger at God for not delivering us in the way we had hoped. We also feel resentment towards those around us who are able-bodied, apparently free from confining circumstances and who seem to be so blessed. We ask 'Where is the victory in this and how can God be glorified in my circumstances?' Added to our hopelessness we have the Job's comforters who come and offer their counsel, but often end up adding condemnation to the burden, instead of bringing any real solace.

It is not that we are unwilling to get out of the rut. We often truly desire to live in victory and will do whatever it takes on our part. We have repented of just about everything, and can probably imagine a few things that we would like to have repented of if only we had committed the sin in the first place! We've bound, loosed, prayed into the generational curse, dealt with every ungodly association, forgiven the whole world, prayed in faith, hope, desperation and we are still in the same mess. Nothing seems to have changed and when we think it couldn't possibly get worse it does! We wonder whether God likes us at all! Does He have any compassion or has He completely abandoned us? It is at times like these when our faith and trust in Him is really tested. We call these 'valley experiences'.

> *'Even though I walk through the valley of the shadow of death, I will fear no evil, for you are with me; your rod and your staff, they comfort me.'*   (Psalm 23:4)

When I was once going through such an experience a friend gave me Psalm 40 to read. Those words were so precious to me and I have clung on to them ever since. What is more, the promises of God have been and are being fulfilled.

> *'I waited patiently for the Lord: he turned and heard my cry. He lifted me out of the slimy pit, out of the mud and mire; he set my feet on a rock and gave me a firm place to stand. He put a new song in my mouth, a hymn of praise to our God. Many will see and hear and put their trust in the Lord.'*

God's promises to us

At this point it might be helpful to take a step back and study some of God's promises to see how they can be applied to the difficult circumstances of our lives. Not only will this help us in our plight, but also give us faith for the future and the ability to focus on what is true victory from God's perspective.

We know that the scripture says *'if God is for us who can be against us?'* (Romans 8:31). Sometimes it doesn't feel that way and we may ask ourselves why this promise is not a reality in our lives now. In response to this I would like to share a passage of scripture that I learnt very early on in my Christian experience.

Romans 8:28 says:

> *'And we know that in all things God works for the good of those who love him, who have been called according to his purpose.'*

Some manuscripts translate the first part of the verse: *'And we know that all things work together for good to those who love God.'* In other words, whatever the circumstances we are in, if we know we are loved by God and have been called according to His purpose, then we can trust Him to work in all our situations for our ultimate good and for His purposes. This means that God can turn every situation around for His glory and our benefit. At this point we have a choice to make. Do we believe this? Can we put our faith in Him and trust His word? Is His promise reliable? If we respond in the affirmative then we need to actively put our faith and trust into this promise of God and say, 'Lord I trust you with the circumstances of my life; You and You alone are capable of redeeming this situation for Your glory and for my benefit.'

A question of perception

It is well worth remembering that our heavenly Father is divine, infinite and almighty. On the other hand we are finite, frail flesh and totally reliant upon Him for every breath. It is by His power we have our being. He is God and His word declares:

> *' "For my thoughts are not your thoughts, neither are your ways my ways," declares the Lord. "As the heavens are higher*

> *than the earth, so are my ways higher than your ways and my*
> *thoughts than your thoughts." '*   (Isaiah 55:8, 9)

No matter how much we think we understand God and His ways, there is always a great mystery interwoven into His dealings with us. He is, after all, God, and His thoughts, purposes and ways of doing things are far beyond ours to understand. There comes a time in all of our lives when we need to acknowledge that God is God and we must lean into Him and trust Him to work out His purposes in our lives.

Trusting God when things go wrong is never easy. I wonder how Moses felt having led the children of Israel out of slavery in Egypt when God brought them to the edge of the Red Sea with the Egyptian army in hot pursuit! (Exodus 14). He was truly caught between the devil and the deep blue sea! Can you imagine the pressure he was under at that time, with the Israelites expressing their discontent and fearful of Pharaoh taking them all back to slavery? Their recapture would mean certain punishment for their attempted escape. In the midst of confusion, fear, frustration and hopelessness the Lord spoke to Moses and gave him a directive to stretch out his staff over the water. I'm sure that when Moses relayed this strategy to the Israelites they were not filled with confidence!

How do you respond on the inside when the enemy is coming after you with hatred in their eyes, you've known their cruelty and have been crushed by their might? You have no weapons, nowhere to hide and no strategy. You know diplomacy is out of the question because historically that approach has failed, and the only way forward is hindered by an expanse of rushing water too deep and strong to wade through. You are now looking to God's 'man of power for the hour' waiting for a mighty plan, only to be told that in response to all the raging circumstances he will point his stick across the water!

To say this was illogical and lacked military wisdom would be the understatement of the year. However, God had spoken to Moses and he obeyed in simple trust and obedience to what he knew to be the Father's voice. It lacked street credibility among the faithful followers but was divine in inspiration. To the amazement of all, the waters parted and provided a way through the sea to safety. What was a safe path to the Israelites, became a route of destruction to the Egyptian army as the seas engulfed and destroyed them.

It appears that God does take us into circumstances that we would not enter into of our own choosing. However, it is in those very situations that He reveals Himself to us in a special way. When we move in obedience to what He requires of us He tests our faith, character and obedience. **The Father is far more concerned about producing the qualities and character of His Son Jesus in our lives than He is about accomplishing tasks through us**.

I am reminded of the hymn by J.H. Sammis:

'When we walk with the Lord
In the light of His Word
What a glory He sheds on the way!
While we do His good will,
He abides with us still,
And with all who will trust and obey.

Trust and obey,
For there's no other way
To be happy in Jesus,
But to trust and obey.

But we never can prove
The delights of His love
Until all on the altar we lay;
For the favour He shows,
And the joy He bestows
Are for them who will trust and obey.'

God sees the whole picture, not just the fraction we see. It takes courage to trust when we cannot see the end from the beginning.

Trusting God

Some years back I was invited to join a ministry based in the South of England. On my first day I arrived to begin work. My responsibilities included developing teaching and being part of the leadership. To my amazement my arrival did not seem a great blessing. In fact, little had been communicated to the staff at this location about my role. I enquired as to who would be my secretary and what office I would occupy. The response was a look of bewilderment and indifference. Eventually I was offered a tiny desk in a busy corridor and informed that there would be no secretary. Nobody from the leadership had time to help me and I began to feel I had made a terrible mistake. The situation was very different to what I had envisaged and I could not see how I was supposed to work in such an environment.

After wasting most of the day hanging around and feeling completely in the way I returned home with the intention of not returning. That night I sought the Lord and was amazed at what He showed and said to me. As I prayed the Lord showed me a white water rapid with fast flowing water over large boulders. Steep banks bordered the torrent of rushing water. I was in a small boat with my hand on the tiller, riding the flow of water and negotiating the rocks to avoid destruction. The Lord then said to me, 'You have learned skilfully to ride the rapids of your life. You have learned to negotiate around dangerous obstacles and avoid being wrecked by the rocks when they appear before you. You have learned to control sufficient to survive, but you do not know where you are going or how to get there; you just know how to survive. Let go of the tiller and allow My hand to take over because I know the destination and the way to it. You must let go and trust Me. Sit in the boat and watch as we ride the waves together and we will not only survive but we will reach My objectives for you. Trust Me, let go and let Me take over.'

I was convinced that God had spoken to me, which gave me faith to see through what the Lord had in store for me. I chose to trust the Lord completely and return and submit myself to the situation. To my delight when I returned I was completely disarmed at the response of the manager of the base who was apologetic, accepting and accommodating! From that point I began a three-year adventure of faith and trust in God. I found myself in the most hilarious, ridiculous, frustrating, bewildering, character-building, healing, intense period of my life. During that time I learned more about myself, and by God's grace was given opportunities to develop in ministry that could not have been made available elsewhere. It pays to trust God even when it seems illogical and proves at times to be 'Doing your head in'. His ultimate work in us is worth its weight in gold.

The ultimate expression of trust in God that I have seen is that of Christ upon the cross. In Luke 23:46 we read the words of our saviour:

> ' "Father into your hands I commit my spirit." When He had said this, He breathed His last.'

This is an incredible statement and action, particularly when everything around Jesus at that time offered no evidence of the Father's presence. There hung Jesus on the cross, beaten beyond recognition at the hands of cruel men. Having felt the presence of His Father leave Him when the sins of the world were put upon Him, He gave His life as a sacrifice for atonement, and had cried *'My God, why have you forsaken me?'* (Mark 15:33).

This was not so much a question to the Father of His actions but a heart-cry of pain and emotion, as for the first time the presence of His Father unable to abide in a sinful environment departed from Him. On the cross Jesus was utterly alone as He endured the rejection of humanity and now the rejection from the Father and the mocking of the demonic. It was at this exact moment when His body was wracked with pain, His emotions torn and tormented and His spirit polluted by an alien condition called sin, that He yielded His life into the hands of one He could not see, could not feel, with no evidence around to trust Him. Jesus yielded His spirit into the hands of one who required all of this from

Him. Believing in the promise of the Father to Him, enabled Him to endure the cross, despising its shame, for the joy that was set before Him. His faith was in the promise which gave hope of better things to come.

We too are called to walk by faith and not by sight. When we focus on the immediate circumstances around us we can so easily become discouraged and overwhelmed by negative thoughts which destroy hope and expectation. However, when we trust the Father and believe His promises to us we will focus on the hope to which He has called us that will enable us to endure with perseverance until that which is promised is fully realised.

Personal responsibility

Whoever and wherever we are, we have an effect on others. The way we respond to the circumstances we find ourselves in challenges others with their own responses to situations. In addition, those who are involved with us can be directly affected by the way we act. For example, if you are bed-ridden it might be members of your family who have to care for you, or you may be a single parent with children looking to you as a role model. As an invalid, it is obvious that if you are resentful, angry and irritable it does not help your carers in their task or make life pleasant for those who have to share the same home. Furthermore, God will be dealing with them and their heart issues through your circumstances. Alternatively, as a single parent, you may feel isolated, alone and resentful of the children who are dependent upon you.

However, God will want to work His character into your life which will in turn influence the children, allowing them to grow up in a secure environment. Others will be watching too – neighbours, family and friends will observe how you respond to the circumstances you are in. Are you always angry, frustrated and resentful, or are you expressing the grace of God and living in His strength? We are talking here about heart attitudes that are forced to the surface when the heat is turned up.

Brokenness yielding quality fruit

Many years ago I met a couple in the USA who were in Christian leadership. The man had a prominent healing ministry but his wife had been in a terrible accident that left her disabled and in need of a lot of attention. Many 'words' and 'prophecies' had been given to them about her recovery, and while the Lord had saved her life from the effect of her condition many times, there had been no improvement whatsoever for over twenty years. As time went by the man's frustration, resentment and anger expressed itself in many different ways, even though he tried his hardest to contain it. The hurt was so apparent that he became very difficult to approach. He was like a prickly hedgehog. Even though his conversation would be scripturally sound, it could be quite dangerous to be near him and many people withdrew from his company. This, in turn, compounded his rejection, which produced more anger and resentment. Ultimately the other leaders of the church had no alternative but to ask him to step down from his position. This further increased his hurt and pain and he became reclusive and angry at the whole church in the area. He began to hold small house meetings in his home with a few faithful followers. There was often an attitude of 'Why aren't you loving me? Why aren't you caring for us? I can survive on my own. We don't need you. Watch to see how God will use us. You will all come to us and apologise eventually.' Unfortunately this just drove him into further isolation. Even though a number of hands reached out and tried to help, he only wanted things on his own terms. It grieved my heart to see someone who had such an anointed ministry shrinking into an embittered pool of pain due to a heart attitude that was too inflexible to flow with God.

On the other hand, I have met some of the bravest, most loving, caring people who live with the most horrendous deformity and incurable diseases. Yet somehow they have allowed the grace of God to flow in and through them and in turn touched other people deeply. It is as if something inside of them has broken and released the very fragrance of Christ. There is a gratitude for the good things they have, rather than a complaint about the things that they do not have. Whilst they experience the frustration, suffering and hurt of their circumstances, which needs continual healing, they have chosen to live in victory and not allow their circumstances to overpower and destroy them. They seek to rise up in Christ and allow the fruit of the Spirit to be manifest in their lives.

An example of this is a couple I have known for some years where the wife is in a wheelchair suffering from multiple sclerosis. Her husband has even prayed for others with the same condition who have been miraculously healed and yet their own circumstances have remained unchanged. However, they are moving prominently in the prophetic and healing ministry, bringing God's love and grace to many. What thrills my heart is to see this woman reaching out and touching others in counsel and pastoral care, ministering gifts of healing into their lives from her wheelchair. This is such a wonderful exemplification of God's grace and mercy. Rather than living in resentment and bitter pain, from their own brokenness they reach out to touch the lives of others and in turn receive great acceptance and admiration for their courage and devotion to the call of God.

Valley experience

Over eleven years ago I found myself in circumstances I would never have chosen whilst pastoring a small church in the South of England. It was a pioneering situation and I was also required to hold a full-time job in order to create sufficient revenue to support my family and invest in the church. One cold, dark January evening I had driven from the city of London to my home and had a sense of foreboding as I entered the house. My wife stood with her bags packed and she spoke the unforgettable words, 'I don't love you any more. I'm in love with someone else and I'm leaving you.' There had been a number of rows over the years and a distancing between us. Initially I thought that this was just another war about to begin, but I soon realised this was for real and that she was going. Following her statement she turned, walked out of the front door and was met at the corner of the road by our worship leader and the two of them went off together.

I returned to the house and in the lounge were my five- and three-year-old daughters and my nine-month-old son. All manner of emotions can arise in such circumstances – panic, fear, shame, self-blame, regret, inadequacy as a husband etc. I comforted the children in their distress and assured them that God would never desert us. Within twenty-four hours I had lost my position as a pastor and rumours spread through the Christian community about my alleged ungodly sexual behaviour. To compound the pain, it seemed that all of the church was running after my former wife and her lover, to be all they could to them in the name of Christ, leaving the children and me to fend for ourselves. Together we faced three years of complete isolation from the Christian community and lived with the imposed disgrace of my circumstances.

There were one or two people who helped and stuck with me through those dark years and to whom I will always be grateful. However, for most of the time, we were alone, isolated and cut off, falsely accused and thrown on the scrap heap for Christian failures. It is virtually impossible to describe the emotions that I experienced throughout that time. I know that I spent a lot of time on my face before God crying out to Him, seeking to do what was right from His perspective, realising that no matter what I did it would be wrong in most people's eyes. I chose in that time to devote myself to my family and we lived on state benefit for a period, taking the occasional church meeting as I operated as an itinerant evangelist. Subsequently, after ongoing negotiations for reconciliation, there followed an ugly divorce and years of loneliness.

Yet in these circumstances God tested me as I have never

been tested before, on financial integrity, on my sexuality, on my heart attitudes towards people who had hurt and wounded me, and on standing for righteousness. All in all it was a period of tremendous breaking, dealing with my arrogance, pride, self-centredness and ambition. I can only testify to the grace of God and my amazement at the way He alone can redeem circumstances and enable us to live in victory in the midst of adversity. Even though the valley of life at that time was dark I knew that He would never leave me. Even though it seemed every human hand had slipped off my life and I felt abandoned, I knew the Father was gripping me tighter in His embrace. I had come to a place of rest, realising that even if I never preached nor achieved anything of significance in this life He was still for me and not against me. His love reached out and would never let me go.

The deep work of God

When we are facing difficult problems in our lives there are a number of things that God will always want to do in us as well as dealing with our circumstances. He will want us to accept Him as God and to be Lord over all that we are. He will want us to trust Him, which means having to release the control of our own lives, because when we are in control we are trusting our own ability, whereas when we relinquish control we have to trust God. He will also want us to rest in Him, to lean into Him, and allow Him to work without our striving and seeking to manipulate Him. It is not so much what God can do through us, but what He can do in us that really counts. Therefore He will always be refining our character and seeking to release the fruit of His Spirit within us.

What took real courage on my part was believing that God was capable of redeeming both my family circumstances and the ministry to which I was called. For me to let go and let things die took enormous courage, faith and willingness. Jesus made it very clear that unless a grain of wheat falls to the ground and dies it will remain a single seed, but if it dies it will bear great fruit (John 12:24–26). I believe that I am now living in the reality of God's fulfilled purpose, having been given by God a beautiful new wife, two additional children and a ministry that touches far more people internationally than I could ever have imagined. All this is by the grace of God alone and a willingness to go God's way rather than my own.

Fight the good fight of faith

There is a place for living faith while in the midst of suffering. We are encouraged by Paul in Ephesians 6:10:

> *'Finally, be strong in the Lord and in his mighty power.'*

In the verses which follow we are encouraged to take our stand against the devil's schemes, to stand our ground and to stand firm wearing the whole armour of God, for we fight against demonic powers who actively work against us. There are without doubt times of intense spiritual warfare, and sometimes having started a good fight we crumble under the ferocity of the enemy's attack. Yet we are repeatedly advised in scripture to stand firm on the ground that we have won, through the might and power of Jesus Christ. If we are actively standing when the enemy attacks us (bearing in mind that the scriptures tell us that greater is He that is within us than he that is in the world) and if we stand in the strength of Christ who is far stronger than the enemy, then we are immovable and he will back off exhausted.

Having done all that we can to minister as the Holy Spirit leads and directs, our final resource is to stand firm on the ground we have claimed. It may be that we are unable to move forward or even sideways, but just have to dig deep and hold on whilst the war rages all around us. In all of this we are told that:

> *'God is our refuge and strength, an ever-present help in trouble.'* (Psalm 46:1)

> *'The Lord is my light and my salvation – whom shall I fear?*
> *The Lord is the stronghold of my life – of whom shall I be*
> *afraid?'*   (Psalm 27:1)

A stronghold is a fortified place of refuge, which doesn't move anywhere. It is a place of safety where we can be protected and feel secure. The Psalmist is saying, 'The Lord is my stronghold, of whom shall I be afraid?' As we stand firm in the stronghold of God we can be assured of victory, even when we are going through difficult circumstances, because we are standing in Christ Jesus.

We also need to look at some of the biblical characters that had to suffer for the name of God. I am thinking specifically of people like Daniel facing the lion's den and Shadrach, Meshach and Abednego who refused to bow down to an idol and were thrown into the furnace. For each one, God redeemed the whole situation and brought glory and honour to His own name, vindicating the oppressed and elevating them to a higher position. However, there were others who stood firm but were not delivered as you might have expected. We can read about them in Hebrews 11:35–38. Some were tortured and refused release, or faced jeers and were flogged. Some were put into chains and imprisoned or stoned. Others were even sawn in two and put to death by the sword. They were destitute, persecuted and mistreated and the writer goes on to say that the world was not worthy of them. Even though they wandered in deserts, mountains, caves and holes in the ground, all of these people were commended for their faith, yet not one of them received what had been promised, at least in this life, because God had something better planned for them.

We also read in Hebrews 5:8 that Jesus, even though He was a son, had to learn obedience through what He suffered. Once made perfect, He became the source of eternal salvation for all who obey Him. Again and again Jesus was tempted not to go the way of the cross. He also suffered for His firm stand of obedience to the Father's will experiencing rejection, misunderstanding, loneliness and hardship.

For us too, God works His character in us through our sufferings. Our focus perhaps should be not so much on the disability or the unjust circumstances we find ourselves in, but on accepting God's plan and purpose for us at that time. In yielding and accepting we learn to rest and trust in Him in a way that we could not have done in any other circumstance. In this way, it is more than possible to live in victory, even in the midst of adversity.

Redeeming the circumstances

I have always found the book of James to be challenging. In fact I recommend that you only read it wearing a crash helmet! He has a way of putting things quite bluntly and without beating around the bush. For example, in James 1:2,

> *'Consider it pure joy, my brothers, whenever you face trials of many kinds.'*

What was his secret? How could he count it pure joy? Most of us want to avoid the trials, look for the easy route and the way of compromise, but James is talking about rejoicing when the difficult times come. He obviously realised that it was only through these trials that the true character of Christ could be manifest in our lives. By trusting God and yielding to His purpose for us His plans could be worked out. May God deliver us from the fear of adverse circumstances and teach us how to embrace them, so that instead of running away we can press through and bring about a great weight of God's glory in our lives.

Some years ago I was in Lagos, Nigeria, ministering at a friend's church. A few weeks before I arrived Muslims had knocked down the church and all that remained was a pile of rubble. They were obviously angry at the clear gospel message that was being proclaimed from this church and sought retaliation. I was so impressed at my friend's faith in these circumstances and encouraged when he assured me that **it is not what happens to us that matters, it's the way we handle what happens to us that really counts**.

The result was that the attack on the church drew immediate media attention, which in turn publicised forthcoming events drawing people, out of curiosity, to see what was going on. When they came and saw the church worshipping amongst the rubble, they heard the gospel and many were saved. In turn they brought their friends and family along who also heard the gospel and were saved. They were so struck by the life, faith and vibrancy of this fellowship.

I returned six months later to hear that the courts had ordered the rebuilding of their church at the expense of those who knocked it down! However, the church had now grown to more than three times its original size and were holding their services in a very large warehouse and also planning an additional building to accommodate all that God was doing. You see, they would have remained a small church of only a thousand people had they not allowed God to work His greater weight of glory through adverse circumstances.

The challenge comes to us – how do we really handle adverse circumstances? Do we want to run away, or do we want to press on in and take hold of that for which Christ Jesus has taken hold of us? Do we moan or look for God's opportunity? If we rest in the Lord and remain faithful to righteousness He will turn all things around for fruitfulness and His glory.

Chapter 4

Mountain Moving
and Problem Pummelling

One of the major keys to victorious Christian living is understanding the principle that the difference between failure and success is to try just one more time. The Bible teaches us that there needs to be tenacity in our character to enable us press on and take hold of that which is rightfully ours. Many Christians live in defeat and failure because they are waiting for something to waft in and land in their laps, rather than realising that what has been secured in the heavenlies needs to be realised in the natural realm. Obstacles which prevent us achieving our goals and objectives need to be understood from God's perspective. It could be that an obstacle is God's way of redirecting us, or it could be that the enemy has put a mountain of opposition before us! God may want **us** to remove the mountain as part of a process of achieving His objectives for us, while developing our faith, trust and growth in spiritual authority.

Everyday Christian experience

> 'I want to know Christ and the power of his resurrection and the fellowship of sharing in his sufferings, becoming like him in his death, and so, somehow, to attain to the resurrection from the dead. Not that I have already obtained all this, or

have already been made perfect, but I press on to take hold of that for which Christ Jesus took hold of me. Brothers, I do not consider myself yet to have taken hold of it. But one thing I do: Forgetting what is behind and straining towards what is ahead, I press on towards the goal to win the prize for which God has called me heavenwards in Christ Jesus.'

(Philippians 3:10–14)

Paul was writing to the Philippian church from a Roman prison while awaiting execution. His whole letter is on the theme of Christian experience and living in victory. He was building the Philippians' confidence in God in the midst of what they had to face on a day-to-day basis.

Paul's own experience in visiting Macedonia can be read in Acts 16, following his dream of a man dressed in Macedonian clothing beckoning him to come and help. Realising this was from God, he and his entourage sailed for Macedonia. They landed at Philippi and met Lydia who was a dealer in purple cloth and a worshipper of God. The Lord opened her heart to the gospel; Paul and his friends were welcomed into her household and the Philippian church had begun!

One day when they were walking to their place of prayer, a slave girl who had a spirit of divination yelled after them, 'These men are servants of the Most High God who are telling you the way to be saved.' Now most people would have been quite flattered by this exclamation but Paul, who saw with the eyes of his heart, understood the torment of this young woman and delivered her from an unclean spirit in the name of Jesus Christ. The owners of the slave girl, realising that their hope of making money through her divination was gone, seized Paul and Silas and dragged them into the market place to face the authorities. As a result they were thrown into prison. Around midnight they were praying and singing hymns to God while the other prisoners listened on. Suddenly there was a violent earthquake and the foundations of the prison were shaken. The prison doors flew open, and everybody's chains fell off. The jailer of course woke up and went to see what was happening.

Realising that the doors were open, he assumed that all the prisoners had escaped and was about to kill himself when Paul shouted out, 'Don't harm yourself, we are all still here.' The jailer called for lights and seeing that everyone was indeed present, he fell trembling before Paul and Silas and cried, 'What must I do to be saved?' They replied, 'Believe on the Lord Jesus Christ and you and your household will be saved.' As they spoke the Word of God to him he found living faith in Jesus Christ and he and his family were immediately baptised. God ultimately redeemed the whole situation. When the authorities came in the morning to talk to Paul and Silas, Paul explained that they were Roman citizens and had been thrown into prison without a fair trial. This struck terror into the hearts of the magistrates who realised that they had broken their own law, so they personally escorted Paul and Silas from prison and requested them to leave the city.

What an amazing story! This is what life is like when we follow the leading of the Holy Spirit and move in obedience to His will and purpose. One day we may plant a church, the next we can minister deliverance; one day we are in prison, the next God saves the jailer, the authorities repent of their unreasonable behaviour and release us from prison. We see that life is a mixture of good and unpleasant circumstances so we must be like Paul who never seemed to give up.

In 2 Timothy 4:6, 7 Paul says,

> *'For I am already poured out like a drink offering, and the time has come for my departure. I have fought the good fight, I have finished the race, I have kept the faith.'*

All those who were once close had deserted him yet he testified that he fought to the end and finished the race that God had set before him.

It is so important that we resolve in our minds to run the race the Lord has marked out for us. In so doing the Father will bring glory to Himself, our lives will be fulfilled and others whose lives we have touched will be blessed.

A lesson to learn

A number of years ago I was serving the Lord in a non-denominational healing ministry based in England. One of my responsibilities was to develop outreach and evangelism, so in this capacity I suggested holding a residential training course which would include a two-week mission in an Eastern European Country. The whole concept was new to the work both at our home base and our Eastern European base, which would have to handle the organisation before we arrived en masse as a team of raw, inexperienced, fearful would-be evangelists.

The first task was to sell the idea to our own people and convince them it was a God thing and that the extra work, inconvenience and risk was worth the effort. The second hurdle was to publicise the event through our existing network of supporters. I hoped to attract more young people than usually came to our events, especially those with a bit of 'get up and go' about them. I needed those willing to look outside themselves and be able to endure the rigours of the course and mission experience.

To my dismay the numbers registering were far lower than I had hoped and a number who were applying did not appear to be the type I was hoping for. As the time for the course start date drew near the problems seemed to mount and I became more discouraged. Except for a few, the staff within the work found it difficult to own the concept of the course as it was so different from what they were used to. I therefore found it hard to get the co-operation required and was met with an ongoing misinterpretation of my instructions. Unfortunately things started being organised and put in place which were contrary to my requirements.

Tension had also risen as to the style of the publicity and the original brochures were scrapped as not being in keeping with the image of the work as a whole. It was difficult for them to accept something which was not usual for them and it was hard for me to accept the status quo. I had to accept the Director's decision and in many ways I became grateful for his trust in me and his willingness to take risks with the project which he personally backed whole-heartedly.

Frustration arose within me and a lot of fear began to grip my heart. Money had now been invested in the project, people were committed to embark on the course, but I did not have enough team leaders within the work either willing or capable to lead the small teams once on mission. I therefore had to call on friends to help who I had worked with previously. In addition our Eastern European base had difficulty encouraging the bi-lingual locals to act as translators to enable communication with local churches in evangelism, etc.

Problem after problem arose just to get this event to take place. Nothing was simple. The flights, local transport for missions and accommodation for teams had been complicated, confused and frustrated, but despite all the upsets, hurdles and disputes, by God's grace alone, the day came when the delegates arrived. Although not everything was in place, I was in faith trusting the Lord for a few miracles.

Having met the delegates I asked each one on the course to introduce themselves and it became apparent that many of them were needy people. They all had the courage, however, to go beyond their known experience and were willing to push themselves further than they had gone before. There were among them the 'get up and go' reasonably together types, but we had also gathered more than our fair share of the very timid, socially dysfunctional, elderly, deeply rejected, hurting folk. One thing in our favour though, was that they all loved God and had the courage and willingness for God to change them.

The teaching and ministry helped the team learn fast and gel together well. What we lacked in talent we made up for in enthusiasm! Quickly the day for departure arrived and we were whisked off to Heathrow to catch our flight to take the world for Jesus. All went well until one of our party lost their passport, while another lost their return ticket and those who wanted to get over their terror of flying stayed close by me. All in all it wasn't a bad start taking the past few weeks into consideration and we were off having resolved these few minor hiccups.

On our arrival we were taken to our accommodation which was reasonable by local standards, but there was only ever sufficient warm water for one person to shower per day (for nearly forty people), one lady found a chicken's foot floating in her soup and an invasion of cockroaches shared our first evening meeting! A few controlled flutters did go through the party, but we were on mission and eventually what we saw happen through these inexperienced, frightened folk was against all odds and quite remarkable.

One church took us to a local youth prison of about 100 hardened, rejected lads who were habitual criminals. The atmosphere was tense as they were brought into the assembly hall with staff and security officers. The local church worship team sang, we did a short simple skit and one of our girls gave her testimony of how she was saved. This described how she hated herself and had become rebellious, but Jesus had come into her life, saved her and set her free to live a meaningful life. I followed that with a short gospel message and a clear explanation about God's grace and the need to repent. Every single person in the hall, except five boys, stood to receive Jesus into their lives and tears flowed as they received the Father's love, forgiveness and acceptance. The team and local church members could hardly believe their eyes so I explained the gospel again, repeating what was required of them in case something had been misunderstood through the translation, but they all wanted to get saved! We left rejoicing, handing them over to the local churches' care and follow-up.

Another small team was placed in an inner city church and two male members had to travel, along with the translator from the church, by cab to their hosts. On arrival they jumped out of the cab and the rear door was slammed shut with the translator's hand trapped in it. The poor man cried out in pain and when they released him he was white-faced and faint with his hand badly cut and swollen. Everyone seemed in a panic unsure what to do when one of our over seventy-year olds discussed with his team-mate how they had been taught to pray for healing on the course, so they said 'Why don't we try that?' They gathered around the injured man asking Jesus to heal the damaged hand and take the pain away. The next morning the translator said he had slept well, the pain had gone and his hand was virtually healed. A miracle had taken place through the hands of men who had no experience of the healing ministry at all.

Many more stories could be told of how, against all odds, demonic resistance and human frailty we pressed on to accomplish the purposes of God. Through the ministry of obedient inexperienced folk, God brought over five hundred people into His kingdom and several miracles of healing took place. There was angelic intervention and a number of local churches were inspired to witness to the lost, having seen what God could do through ordinary men and women, many of whom would not be considered right material for such situations.

Our experience is that when we hear God and walk in obedience to Him, He is faithful to work with us. As we press in against all the odds God will always find a way to accomplish His purposes and bring glory to Himself. He also works character and maturity into our lives, develops faith and gives us a great sense of accomplishment, purpose and fulfilment. I have seen this process repeated again and again down through the years.

Removing obstacles

Paul said to the Philippian church, *'I press on to take hold of that for which Christ Jesus has taken hold of me'* (Philippians 3:12). In other words he came across circumstances that in every way caused him to want to give up, but he kept his focus on what God had called him to. He was reminded that his first priority was to fulfil what he was called for and that no matter what was before him causing difficulties he was going to press on, to press in, to stand on, to stand firm, choosing to allow God to fulfil His plans for his life and not give up.

I wonder what the obstacles are in your way today. What it is that hinders you from pressing on and pressing in? Are you going to look at it and allow this mountain of opposition to overwhelm you, hinder you, frustrate and defeat you? Or are you going to press on towards the goal, to win the prize for which God has called you heavenward in Christ Jesus?

It is interesting to note that Zechariah 4:6, which we quote so often, is in the context of removing a mountain of opposition from before Zerubbabel:

> *'... "Not by might nor by power, but by my Spirit" says the Lord Almighty.'*

Verse 7 continues,

> *'What are you O mighty mountain? Before Zerubbabel you will become level ground. Then he will bring out the capstone to shouts of "God bless it! God bless it!"'*

The story of Ezra is simple – he had led a remnant of some 50,000 Israelites back from captivity in Babylon to Jerusalem for the purpose of rebuilding the temple. However, work had stopped due to God's people becoming discouraged at the opposition, criticism and hindrance of the local people. As time passed by they grew used to not progressing with their work and settled in to their circumstances of unfulfilled dreams and underachievement.

If we are not careful it can be easy to justify our failures and lost opportunities just like this remnant did. They started well, full of faith and enthusiasm but soon began to let the vision fade and settle for less than God's best. For fourteen years the work remained incomplete until God began to stir the hearts of the prophets Zechariah and Haggai to proceed. As these prophets spoke the word of the Lord into the situation the hearts of the people began to stir and respond to God. They again began to move in faithful obedience and started to rebuild the temple. However, as expected, the obstacles reappeared and criticism, threat, lies and accusation came from local troublemakers but this time instead of submitting to the circumstances they chose to press on. The enemy opposition increased but God's people were now determined and they continued to build. As a result they saw the Spirit of God go before them and turn the circumstances around and the mountain of opposition they had experienced became as level ground. The opposition was silenced and the work on the temple was completed.

God will always find a way where there is no way!

Likewise we have to keep pressing on in obedience to God's plan and purpose for us and as we continue to do so the Spirit of the Lord will level the mountains. It is only when we stop and look at the mountain, try to negotiate around it, or withdraw and go backwards, that we are in defeat.

Jesus said in Matthew 17:20,

> '...I tell you the truth, if you have faith as small as a mustard seed, you can say to this mountain, "Move from here to there" and it will move. Nothing will be impossible for you.'

On that occasion the mountain was a powerful demon inside a young boy which the disciples seemed incapable of removing. Their problem was unbelief and fear of failure but Jesus rebuked the demon and it came out of the boy and he was healed from that moment.

Another time we read in Matthew 21:21,

> 'Jesus replied, "I tell you the truth, if you have faith and do not doubt, not only can you do what was done to the fig-tree, but also you can say to this mountain, 'Go throw yourself into the sea,' and it will be done. If you believe, you will receive whatever you ask for in prayer."'

The disciples had seen Jesus curse a fig tree and watched it wither from its roots. They were amazed and yet Jesus said, with great emphasis, that in His name we can speak to mountains and they will be removed from before us.

At this point we are faced with a challenge – why don't we begin to speak to the mountains in our lives? We can begin to command the obstacles that hinder us achieving God's objectives for us, making them become as level ground. In this way we wage warfare in the spiritual realm in Jesus' mighty name. In faith we can bind the demonic that seeks to resist us because that is what Jesus promised! He will always find a way where there is no way.

> *'If you have faith and do not doubt, ... you can say to this mountain, "Go throw yourself into the sea," and it will be done.'*

All we need is faith the size of a mustard seed to move a mountain. We don't need a mountain of faith to move a mustard seed! Living faith comes from God and it is His divine enabling which achieves His plans and purposes through us.

> *'Now to Him who is able to do immeasurably more than all we ask or imagine, according to His power that is at work in us, to Him be glory ... '*   (Ephesians 3:20)

Why not ask the Father today for His enabling to move on from where you are now to where the Lord is calling you to be? His power working through you will accomplish His plan and purpose for your life, which in turn will bring great glory to Him. Go for it – you have nothing to lose, but everything to gain.

Realised dreams

When I was first saved I would lie on my bed and imagine what it would be like to preach to large crowds of people. In my mind's eye I could see many people coming to faith in Christ, being delivered of the demonic, miraculously healed and filled with the Holy Spirit. There was one slight problem however – I was in the midst of a nervous breakdown and incapable of being anywhere where there were more than a few other people! In fact, I was too afraid to step outside the front door of my home for over twelve months. These fears were crippling and life-controlling, and they brought with them shame, humiliation and torment.

Some time later Jesus miraculously healed me and I began training as a minister of the gospel. Having graduated from Christian Life College in London I began to pastor in the South of England. One day I was invited to speak at a Bible college, during which time I shared a meal with a number of students from Africa. Over the meal they asked if I had ever been to their country to which I replied 'No' but said that I had always wanted to go. I was a little bemused to find myself saying that, because I had no intention of ever going to Africa and was looking to retract my statement, when they replied that they could open up possibilities for me to minister in their country. I replied 'Yes I would love to come – I am sure the Lord is in this' but whilst my mouth was saying that, my head was shaking and I was thinking 'No'! However, the course was set and I was soon on my way to do an evangelistic tour in an African country.

I spent many hours asking the Lord to release me from this, feeling sure He had got the wrong person. I reminded Him of how I didn't like the heat, mosquitoes, snakes, spiders or lizards, and that I had a young family and it wasn't right to leave them, a ministry and a business. I even tried to speak to others to gain their godly counsel in the hope that they would persuade me to cancel the arrangements, but they kept affirming that this was the will of God. The obstacles to overcome were unbelievable – there was trouble with visas and airline tickets, the arrangements were being changed on a daily basis and I became extremely frustrated feeling sure that this must be God's way of telling me that I wasn't to go! Eventually, however, I found myself on a plane, flying far away from home, convinced that God really didn't like me anyway and that I might never return to see my family again! When I arrived it was worse than I had anticipated and I suffered from severe culture shock.

I ministered at a couple of meetings in the main city that went very well and was then transported to a town in the interior. Once there I was horrified to find that God could make such ugly creatures with so many legs, and I couldn't understand why they all seemed to want to come and have a look at me! I clearly remember one occasion when I was standing on a platform in the open air and as the evening drew on a rather large lizard came up and shared the stage with me. I thought that if I stamped my feet in a not-too-obvious way perhaps it would frighten the lizard away, but in fact it drew its attention and it came even closer, at which point I started my Fred Astaire impression! I think the people thought I was dancing in the spirit, but in actual fact I was having a panic attack, running around looking for an exit whilst trying not to lose too much dignity! Later that evening I went back to my hotel room crying out to God and wondering what was the best means of escape from this country. Perhaps if I jumped off the balcony and broke my leg they would ship me back to England – but I'm not very brave when it comes to pain, so I thought better of that idea.

During that night I fought with the demonic in my room. With the hotel's electricity down, the powers of evil just came in at me, works of witchcraft were being projected towards me, which lurked menacingly around seeking to torment me with fears of all kinds. Knowing that the town was steeped in active witchcraft I began to realise that our evangelistic efforts had started to upset those who love to dabble in spiritual darkness. The inhabitants of this town claimed that 365 different demons guarded their area – one for each day of the year. Blood sacrifice was made each day in the town centre to the god of the day, so I was soon made aware of the strength of their power plus their hatred of me and the message I carried.

Through the night I applied the spiritual warfare lessons I had learnt over the years. I realised that I couldn't know victory unless I started fighting so I began to wage serious warfare in the might and name of Jesus Christ. I prayed, pleading the blood of Jesus over me and commanded the demons to leave my room. I applied anointing oil in my room, reconsecrating it and dedicating it to the Lord, declaring the enemy unable to cross the boundaries I had set. The battle raged for some time as I stood my ground in the strength of the Holy Spirit. Eventually peace came, the presence of the Lord filled the room and I slept soundly for the rest of the night.

As I lay on my bed the following day the Holy Spirit took me and, as it were, transported me inside the building where we had been holding the meetings. From the back of this church a very large lizard-like creature began to walk towards me, intending to devour me. In this dream-like state I rebuked the enemy and commanded it to go in the name of Jesus. I have to say it took every ounce of courage to even squeak the words out, let alone speak with a strong authoritative voice. Instead of roaring like a lion I bleated like a sheep. Nonetheless, at the name of Jesus (no matter how feeble it sounded to me), the creature turned away from me, went down through the ground which was then sealed over. Before I had a chance to recover, a very large spider-like creature began coming towards me from the back of the building, and that too was seeking to devour me. I repeated the process, rebuking it in the name of Jesus Christ and commanding it to go. It went the same way, down through the ground, which again was sealed over.

At this point I woke from my dream as the tour co-ordinator entered the room. I enquired about the history of the building in which I was ministering and he informed me that it had been given to the church by the government. I have little insight into governments, but sufficient to know that they rarely give anything away, so I pushed for more information. The co-ordinator told me that nobody else wanted it as it was built on an ancient sacrificial ground and people were afraid to buy it, so it was given to the church! The church had consecrated the building, but to my co-ordinator's knowledge the land had never been reclaimed for the Lord. I therefore assumed the Lord was showing me that there were still demonic rights on the land which were affecting the church in an adverse way.

Up to this point I had not seen any significant move of God in this church. In fact I was deeply disappointed with the poor results from our efforts as people were not coming to faith in Jesus and there were no healings. Armed with this new information we set to prayer and together we began to wage warfare in Jesus' name, binding the enemy's control over the church through its rights on the land, and forbidding the demonic from being active while we were there, no matter what rights they claimed. We said we were there under almighty God's command and they needed to submit to His authority exercised through us in Jesus' name. That evening and on subsequent evenings we saw the power of God move in a tremendous way as people were saved, healed and delivered. One lady with a withered hand stretched it out, was prayed for and it became whole.

Another remarkable testimony during our meetings there was of an elderly man who was obviously finding the whole environment of faith difficult. Under God's anointing I laid hands on him and spoke a blessing into his life. He knew no English and I did not speak his language. I asked God to give him peace and to draw this man back to himself. I then moved on through the crowd ministering to other people. The next evening there was great excitement around this same old man, who was in fact one of the town elders. The ministers of the church asked if I was happy for him to speak a few words, as the Lord had touched him in a special way. Through an interpreter I understood the man to say 'I am an elder of this town, a Muslim and a worshipper of ancestral spirits. Every night since I was very young, demons have come to torment me and make me do things I did not want to do. They filled me with fear and caused me great pain. I came last night just to see what was going on and this preacher came and put his hand upon my head. I felt something had happened and when I returned home I went to bed and for the first time for as long as I can remember no demons came to torment me during the night and my fears have gone. I believe that this man's God is the most powerful and I want to follow him.' This dear old man gave his life to Christ and was never the same again. The crowd went wild with excitement and began to sing, shout, clap and dance in celebration. I took the microphone and led the people in a time of praise, during which I began to jump up and down on the platform declaring that 'Jesus makes me so happy I could jump for joy.' To my amazement 3,000 others in the congregation began to do the same and we continued worshipping Jesus in this unconventional way for some time. I thought at first the Shakena glory of God was filling the place, but soon realised that it was only dust!

My driver later informed me that during the meeting he had been sitting next to an elderly man who seemed most unimpressed with the whole affair until I began to jump up and down on the platform. Apparently he turned to my driver and said with wide-open eyes. 'If there is a god who can make a white man jump up and down with joy then He must be the all-powerful God who can do the impossible.' He instantly gave his heart to Jesus and confessed Him to be Lord of his life! Amazing things happen when God breaks through. This may well be the first person won to Christ while doing the pogo!

The following day I drove to a major city where there was a very large conference taking place. The site held twenty thousand people and I was sharing the platform with some eminent international ministers so I felt very humbled and privileged to be there. That evening I was invited to minister and the Holy Spirit came in power when I gave the word and invited those seeking Christ to come forward. People came forward in droves and I led them in a prayer for salvation, ministering healing and deliverance from the platform. God moved among the people and many were healed, delivered and filled with the Holy Spirit. As I sat down in my chair on the platform while the conference leader took over the meeting, I looked out at the expanse of people. Suddenly I remembered the dream I had had so many years before, lying on my bed in the midst of a nervous breakdown – it was the same picture of crowds getting saved, healed, delivered and filled with the Holy Spirit.

The plans and purposes of God for my life were being fulfilled and I sat weeping with deep gratitude in my heart at the faithfulness of God, but amazed at the grace that He had given me to be able to press on and battle through the obstacles along the way.

The road at times had been painful and often my courage had failed and I was thrown back upon the Lord for strength, wisdom and ability. However, God is faithful and always keeps His promises if we only remain faithful and are determined to obey. We rarely achieve God's objective if we choose to stay in the realm of comfort and convenience.

Paul said,

> *'Press on to take hold of that for which Christ Jesus has taken hold of you. Forget what is behind and strain towards what is ahead. Press on towards the goal to win the prize for which God has called us heavenward in Christ Jesus.'*

Don't give up. Speak to the mountains and they will become as level ground, then move into all that God has for you in Christ Jesus. Remember, **you will never know victory until you have been in a battle**.

Chapter 5

Taking the
Head Off Your Giant

We are witnessing in these days a dramatic move of the Holy Spirit working to revive the church in preparation for its end time work. Whilst God is pouring out His blessing of joy and celebration and drawing us into closer intimacy, He is also anointing His church with great power to achieve His objectives. The enemy, however, would seek to resist God's mighty army at every opportunity. We are promised in scripture however, that the gates of hell will not prevail against it (Matthew 16:18).

There are two levels at which we should consider God's activity and the enemy's counter-attack – first corporately, and secondly individually. There are obvious giants in the land that we face collectively, such as the surge of the occult and New Age interest, the rise of Islam within our cities, the onslaught of materialism and immorality. Even within the church we face Pharisaism, religiosity and the Jezebelic spirit. However, before we can begin to take the giants in our land and within the church corporate, we must, as followers of Jesus Christ, first begin to deal with the giants in our individual lives. The giants that have held us back and controlled our lives are our fears, depression, lust, family problems, unresolved sin issues, bondages, sickness, rejection and rebellion, etc. It is only when we as individuals within the church tackle the giants we personally face that we can corporately be free enough, strong enough and have suffic- ient faith and experience to tackle the giants in the land collectively.

In 1 Samuel 17 we read the story of David and Goliath. While this is a well-known story and many of us will have heard it preached many times, it is worth taking the time to consider the truths contained in this passage and apply them to our lives. First of all, we need to consider the situation we read in verse 3–11 of how God's army occupied one hill and the enemy, the Philistines, occupied another hill, and there was a valley between them. This passage continues to describe the Philistine champion, Goliath, and goes into great detail describing his size, weaponry and reveals his daily challenge to God's army which was to invite them to offer up their champion to engage with him in battle. The loser and his army would become the subjects of the victors. With this challenge he defied the ranks of Israel and the result was that God's army was crippled with fear. We read in verse 20 that daily God's people got into their battle posi- tions and shouted the war cry but never engaged in the battle.

How true this is of us and how this is reflected within the church – we are on one hill and the enemy is on another with a valley between us. Daily the enemy taunts and challenges us but we do not respond. We remain in our isolated positions in the safety of our hillside, churches within their buildings and individual believers in their homes, all just shouting the war cry. As has been stated before in this book you'll never know victory until you've been in a battle, and there is so much unrealised blessing for God's people if they would only rise up and engage the enemy in battle. We have so many promises from God's word and with these we shout the war cry, sing the songs of victory, but fail to dislodge the enemy from his stronghold in our lives, within the church and in our land.

We next see in the story that young David arrives bringing

bread for his older brothers who were in Saul's army. When he arrived and saw the situation that God's people, when challenged, ran away in great fear, something of anger and indignation rose within his heart. He saw the disgrace upon God's people, the humiliation of cowardice and defeat in their lives even before the battle had begun. When Eliab, David's older brother, heard him speaking with the men he became really angry with David and asked him why he had come to the battle line and who was looking after the sheep in the desert that he was responsible for. He accused him of being conceited and wicked of heart and that he had only come to watch the battle. It is interesting to note the reaction of people when God raises up prophets to highlight the condition of the church. This is done not so much as to criticise and humiliate the church, but rather to give opportunity for repentance, to receive God's grace and to inspire to greater things. Yet very often the church's response as revealed throughout history, is one of anger and resentment tending to reject the word of the Lord with proud and hard hearts.

Ways the enemy attacks God's people

1. *Intimidation* (1 Samuel 17:4–7)

> *'A champion named Goliath, who was from Gath, came out of the Philistine camp. He was over nine feet tall. He had a bronze helmet on his head and wore a coat of scale armour of bronze weighing five thousand shekels; on his legs he wore bronze greaves, and a bronze javelin was slung on his back. His spear shaft was like a weaver's rod, and its iron point weighed six hundred shekels. His shield-bearer went ahead of him.'*

These verses give a graphic description of the size and capability of Goliath. What this does is intimidate the observer. So often we gaze looking at the giant in our lives and become intimidated by its apparent enormity. The longer we look at it the bigger it seems to become. When this situation grips our hearts we can become overwhelmed with what I call 'the spirit of the grasshopper'. I find this in Numbers 13:30–33. Here we read how Joshua and Caleb were reporting back to Moses what they had encountered in their reconnaisance of the land of Canaan. We know that the twelve spies went in and ten returned full of fear. Two spies, Caleb and Joshua, returned full of faith in the promises of God, which is illustrated in verse 30 where Caleb silenced the people and said *'we should go up and take possession of the land for we can certainly do it.'* The response of the ten spies who had gone into the land with them was *'we can't attack these people they are stronger than we are.'* It said elsewhere there were giants in the land and they had spread a bad report to the rest of God's people, exaggerating the situation to the point where they said that the land they explored devoured those living in it. All the people we saw there were of great size (verse 32). They continued in verse 33 to say, *'we seemed like **grasshoppers** in our own eyes **and we looked the same to them'.** This is just what happens to us – the more we look at the enemy the bigger he becomes – our imagination takes over and he fills us with intimidation of himself.

2. The enemy challenges our spiritual authority
(1 Samuel 17:10, 23)

> *'Then the Philistine said, "This day I defy the ranks of Israel! Give me a man and let us fight each other." ... As he was talking with them, Goliath, the Philistine champion from Gath, stepped out from his lines and shouted his usual defiance, and David heard it.'*

Daily Goliath defied the ranks of Israel. He appeared unafraid, unaffected and unimpressed by the army that faced him. He saw that he could intimidate them, so grew in confidence within himself. It seems to me that the world is not mad at the church but rather it is bored with it! They have seen and heard the church sing its war cry and songs of victory, but they look at the reality and the condition of our lives and see little to be challenged by. We, as a result, feel their disdain, recognise their challenge and back off. Instead of the enemy defying us, it is time we began to defy the enemy and not accept his resistance to achieving God's objectives through us.

Some years ago I led a team to Estonia just at the time that the Iron Curtain had come down. We were engaged in evangelism, teaching, training and ministry among the Russian speaking people in Talin. During our time there a friend had asked us to collect some books that had been translated into Russian and were being printed in Talin. These books were vital to Russian-speaking believers and our responsibility was to get them from the printer.

This seemed an easy job initially until we arrived at the printers to be told that the place was closed for the day due to the changing currency taking place at that time and the person there was not authorised to release anything. We tried to negotiate through our translator but the lady representing the printers kept saying, 'No, you cannot have the books.' My friend and I kept smiling at the lady and speaking in tongues while the translator insisted that we have the books. She looked at us somewhat bemused, continued to say 'No' firmly and shake her head with determination while she went behind the counter and lifted up the boxes containing our books. We continued to speak in tongues, smile at the lady as we took hold of the boxes and hastily left. The lady, however, was still shaking her head and saying that we could not have the books as we left the premises with the books in our arms!

I believe this was a typical example of spiritual warfare. The books were ours, they had been paid for, but there was demonic resistance to them being released and distributed to those who needed them. It would have been so easy to have accepted this lady's first answer and walked away discouraged. However, we believed it was right to press in and not take 'no' for an answer.

3. *The enemy fills us with fear* (1 Samuel 17:11, 24)

> 'On hearing the Philistine's words, Saul and all the Israelites were dismayed and terrified. ... When the Israelites saw the man, they all ran from him in great fear.'

The response of the army of God in the face of Goliath and the Philistine army was that they were dismayed and terrified. They were filled with great fear and they ran from the situation. Our heavenly Father never intended us to fear the kingdom of darkness, rather that the kingdom of darkness should fear us. The Bible tells us in 1 John 4:4, that *'greater is He that is within us* [the Holy Spirit] *than he that is within the world* [the enemy].' And yet the enemy in so many of our lives has intimidated us and challenged our authority thus rendering our hearts fearful and unwilling to engage in battle.

Many years ago when the Lord first began to call me into healing and deliverance I had a series of horrific nightmares. During the night I would have a recurring dream in which I would be chased by an invisible monster. It was dark all around me and as I tried to run away from the monster I could not move. The only way I could escape was to turn around and run backwards but that would mean having to face the monster. I would wake up screaming and distressed. The dreams were very real and it came to the point that I dreaded going to bed at night for fear of the nightmare. I realised the enemy was seeking to put fear of him in my heart and I sought the Lord for help. Jesus simply reminded me of my authority in His name, which I knew theologically, but obviously was not using it experientially until one night. The dream began as usual with the monster coming towards me and I turned to run but found I couldn't move. My only action was to face the monster. In my dream I asked the Lord for His help and I tried to rebuke this monster with an authoritative roaring rebuke in the name of Jesus, but all that came out was a squeak like a mouse, yet I managed to tell the monster to go in Jesus' name. Instantly the darkness dispelled, the monster disappeared and I woke up this time, not with dread and fear but with peace. I realised just how powerful the name of Jesus really is. It was not so much an authoritative roar, which I couldn't muster up because of my weakness, but it was the name of Jesus that caused the enemy to flee. The scriptures tell us that the demons know the name of Jesus and when they hear it they scream in terror.

4. *The enemy conditions us for defeat* (1 Samuel 17:16)

> *'For forty days the Philistine came forward every morning and evening and took his stand.'*

We read here that the enemy had been taunting God's army for forty days both morning and evening. The enemy took his stand and defied the army of Israel. It seems every time we seek to move in advancement against the enemy or to achieve the objectives that God has for us, the enemy pounces and robs us continually of the blessing of the Lord. If this happens again and again we become conditioned for defeat and bondage and say 'that's the way I am.' We learn to accommodate into our lives things that God has not designed us for or desires us to carry and we feel hopeless and without confidence.

It is, of course, also true that the more we hear something the more we will tend to believe it. Also if we live our lives accommodating our giants we will come to accept them and become conditioned to defeat. This is, of course, just where the enemy has got many of us, to the point where we do not expect breakthroughs or victory anymore. We do not expect healing; we do not expect resource provision; we do not expect to experience the blessing of God. We have been gripped by a spirit of poverty that robs us of the abundance of God and we have become conditioned to small-mindedness and unbelief in our lives.

One of the frustrations and disappointments that I experience in this country of Britain is the conditioning of the church for unbelief, doubt, and scepticism. There is, by and large, little faith in the promises of God for us and therefore we live under a shroud of death and defeat, which makes a hostile environment for seeds of living faith to flourish and grow.

5. *Division* (1 Samuel 17:28)

> *'When Eliab, David's oldest brother, heard him speaking with the men, he burned with anger at him and asked, "Why have you come down here? And with whom did you leave those few sheep in the desert? I know how conceited you are and how wicked your heart is; you came down only to watch the battle." '*

David's brothers were quite happy sitting on the hillside in the safety zone daily shouting the war cry, daily getting into their battle positions. Everything was all right until David came along and stirred things up. He challenged their complacency, he provoked them with his exasperation of their condition, to the point where they burned with anger at him. I have had said to me that 'we would like the Holy Spirit to move more freely in the midst of us but He does tend to cause division.' It is not the Holy Spirit who causes division as He brings with Him the life of God, the love and power of the Father. It is the stubbornness of human hearts, the pride, arrogance and complacency of people that resist the Holy Spirit who cause division. So often down through church history God has raised up men and women with a fire in their hearts to proclaim the truth of the kingdom of God in the midst of a complacent church. All too often the church has rejected these as misfits or rebels, when in actual fact they were prophets of God. The result for those rejected was having to set up new works that grew into denominations, or operate independently of the local churches to reach the lost for Christ, feed and clothe the poor and touch the nations with the kingdom of God.

I remember many years ago I was asked to lead a mission in a town where a number of churches had gathered to host it. The day before the event was over, having seen many young people come to faith in Jesus Christ, I overheard one deacon saying to another, 'I can't wait until he goes so we can get back to normal again.' God has not called us to live in the normal, the complacent or the safety zone. He has called us to advance the kingdom of God. Unfortunately there will always be those who will resist the work of the Spirit of God.

Ways to overcome the enemy

Many of us have struggled in our own strength down through the years, but now we recognise that we need the Holy Spirit to help us. God is calling us to rest in Him, to deliver us from our sense of failure and to set us free from the stigma of being slaves to sin, controlled by areas where the enemy has influence. It is time for us to allow the Lord to restore the years that the locusts have eaten (Joel 2:25).

1. David got a clear perspective of the enemy's attack

While the army of God looked out from their hillside stronghold at the enemy, they saw Goliath standing arrogantly displaying his weaponry. They also heard the voice of Goliath shattering their peace and the more they looked at him the larger he got. The larger he got, the smaller they felt. It was, however, different for David. Even though he was just a boy he had spent much of his life looking after sheep on the hillside during the nights. I believe that while he was alone, without distraction, he would have had time to get to know his God. While looking up at the starry sky wondering at the beauty and enormity of God's creation, the bigger God became. The Psalms reveal David's heart, insight and understanding of God. They reveal his perspective of life, and during these times of intimacy with the Father he became more aware of God's strength, love, compassion and faithfulness. When the time came for him to confront the enemy, the enemy was not so big to him in comparison with the size of his God.

A pastor friend of mine in Nigeria once told me of an occasion when he was in a city centre and came across two young men fighting. He went between the two of them and separated the brawl. One of the young men turned on him and pointed his ring at my friend saying, 'Don't touch me or I'll get you with my Juju ring' (Juju being a form of witch-craft practised in that part of the world). At this point my friend began to laugh, which seemed to anger the young man even more and he said, 'Don't you laugh at Juju, there's power in Juju.' My friend then began to laugh uncontrollably which made the young man ask, 'Why are you laughing?' My friend replied, 'Your god is so small he has to live in a ring! My God cannot be contained even within the universe. Do you think I am afraid of a god that has to live in a ring?' So many people are afraid of what the devil is doing. It is time to get a clear perspective of God, which will enable us to get a clear perspective of the enemy without fear or intimidation. The Bible says in Ephesians 6:12:

> *'For our struggle is not against flesh and blood, but against the rulers, against the authorities, against the powers of this dark world and against the spiritual forces of evil in the heavenly realms.'*

In Colossians 2:15 we read:

> *'And having disarmed the powers and authorities, he made a public spectacle of them, triumphing over them by the cross.'*

In 2 Kings 6:15–17 we read how the servant of Elisha was afraid when he saw the enemy army with its horses and chariots surrounding the city. Elisha's response was to tell him not to be afraid, and he declared that those who are with us are more than those who are with them. Elisha prayed and the Lord opened up the eyes of the servant and he saw all over the surrounding hills around Elisha were horses and chariots of fire. It is not so much how big the enemy is, it is how great our God is.

2. *David aggressively went after the enemy* (1 Samuel 17:32)

> *'David said to Saul, "Let no-one lose heart on account of this Philistine; your servant will go and fight him."'*

David didn't wait for the enemy to attack him. He realised that the best means of defence was to attack. It might therefore be a good tactic of ours, instead of being on the defensive and reactive, to take a good look at our lives, recognising the hell and the bullying of Satan all around us. We should then say, 'Enough is enough!' and begin to exercise our authority in Christ Jesus to expel him from his position.

3. Past experiences prepare for the present
(1 Samuel 17:34–37)

> 'But David said to Saul, "Your servant has been keeping his father's sheep. When a lion or a bear came and carried off a sheep from the flock, I went after it, struck it and rescued the sheep from its mouth. When it turned on me, I seized it by its hair, struck it and killed it. Your servant has killed both the lion and the bear; this uncircumcised Philistine will be like one of them, because he has defied the armies of the living God. The LORD who delivered me from the paw of the lion and the paw of the bear will deliver me from the hand of this Philistine." Saul said to David, "Go, and the LORD be with you." '

David, having volunteered to take Goliath on, was brought into Saul's presence. He was obviously a little concerned to see such a young man taking on such a fierce opponent, but David assured him that as a shepherd boy he had had to face lions and bears while he looked after the sheep on the hillside. He believed that if God helped him then, He would surely help him now. Our heavenly Father never calls us to battles we are unprepared for. All our past experience enables us to contend with what the enemy would throw at us today. Every battle we go through increases our calibre as a warrior in the kingdom of God.

It is not only for battles that God prepares us through life's experiences, but also for handling the responsibilities that He gives to us. I praise God for the years I worked in the construction industry and the years running my own business, for the skills learned, the pressures endured, the responsibilities, planning and the risks taken. These have added to all that I learned at Bible College and in pastoral work, enabling us to do what we do today. There is no education wasted in the kingdom of God.

4. David couldn't fight in someone else's armour
(1 Samuel 17:38–40)

> *'Then Saul dressed David in his own tunic. He put a coat of armour on him and a bronze helmet on his head. David fastened on his sword over the tunic and tried walking around, because he was not used to them. "I cannot go in these," he said to Saul, "because I am not used to them." So he took them off. Then he took his staff in his hand, chose five smooth stones from the stream, put them in the pouch of his shepherd's bag and, with his sling in his hand, approached the Philistine.'*

The truth is that we cannot be someone else, but only the best that we can be. However, there is often a pressure on us to be cloned into someone else or to model ourselves on heroes of the past. While it is good to take on the qualities of these people, God has given us an uniqueness and an individuality and it is this that God will use for His own ends to bring glory to Himself. Unfortunately the enemy does bring pressure to bear, which causes us to be dissatisfied with who we are. This is a lie of the devil and we need to embrace who we are as unique and blessed of God. When we express tones of dissatisfaction with ourselves we are in fact saying to God that He has made a mistake in His creation. We need to embrace who we are in Christ and begin to allow the Holy Spirit to enable us to love ourselves and appreciate who we are.

Our churches operate with structures that can be a blessing in some respects but at the same time can cripple, hinder and frustrate the development of gifting and ministry, thus limiting what God can do. For example, when I first felt called to ministry I was informed that I would have to go to

Bible College and become a pastor, which was the system. No matter what my gifting or calling, the only real expression of serving God full-time was to become a pastor in the mould of the denomination.

I cannot count the number of men and women I have counselled over the years who have been frustrated and crushed, with their natural calling squashed, as they were squeezed into a system that stifled them rather than developed their uniqueness and gifting. We just cannot wear someone else's armour for we will then become encumbered. I believe that God is breaking down structures today that do not really serve His purposes or that limit the life of God and hinder gifted people. God is replacing them with more biblically based structures that release life, rather than constraint, so the gifting and calling of men and women can flow into effective ministry.

5. *David spoke the word of faith* (1 Samuel 17:45)

David not only spoke the word of truth, he acted upon it in faith.

> *'But do you want to know, O foolish man, that faith without works is dead?'* (James 2:20 NKJ)

We need to lay claim to the promises of God's word and declare its truth into our circumstances. Not only this, but we need to act upon them in faith. David went up to the giant and said:

> *'You come against me with sword, spear and javelin, but I come against you in the name of the Lord Almighty, the God of the armies of Israel whom you have defied. This day the Lord will hand you over to me and I will strike you down and cut off your head. Today I will give the carcasses of the Philistine army to the birds of the air and the beasts of the earth and the whole world will know that there is a God in Israel. All those gathered here will know that it is not by sword or spear that the Lord saves, for the battle is the Lord's and he will give all of you into our hands.'*

Goliath cursed David by his own gods and insulted him so that the air was filled with his abuse and his defiance of God. The Philistine moved towards David to attack him and David ran quickly towards the battle line to meet with him. He reached into his bag and took out a stone, slung it and struck the Philistine on the forehead. The stone knocked him off balance and he fell face down onto the ground. Probably because of the weight of his own armour, he found it difficult to get back up onto his feet and certainly he was not quick enough to fend off the nimble-footed David, who took the sword of the giant and with it sliced off his head.

There are two interesting reactions to this. First of all, when the Philistines saw that their hero was dead they were gripped with fear and turned and ran. Having seen a shepherd boy kill their champion they hardly felt a match for an army of such valiant men.

The other reaction is that of the Israelite army. When they saw what David had done their hearts were not filled with fear any more. Instead they were filled with faith and courage and they ran after the Philistines and pursued them. It is amazing what a little victory can do in our lives. Once we begin to have victory in our lives, the enemy sees and is filled with fear and his stronghold begins to diminish. A little success gives us confidence and the courage to continue.

In Mark 11:22–23 we are told:

> ' "Have faith in God," Jesus answered. "I tell you the truth, if anyone says to this mountain, 'Go, throw yourself into the sea,' and does not doubt in his heart but believes that what he says will happen, it will be done for him." '

Faith is a vital key to releasing the power of the kingdom of God. Jesus told us to speak to the mountains of enemy obstacles and resistance, to rebuke them and command them to clear out of the way. It is a good time to begin to speak to the mountain or the giant in your life and begin to take off its head.

Concluding Word

Life is just not easy at times! The sooner we realise that we live in a battle zone, the sooner we can stop living in defeat. God has provided all the resources for us to overcome, to rise up, take some control and exercise authority over our lives and circumstances. He has made it clear that we are in a spiritual warfare and in this battle we have three main enemies; the world, the flesh and the devil. But Jesus has overcome all of these at the cross. We therefore have the right, as sons of God living in Christ, to exercise all authority in the power of the Holy Spirit, to have victory and remain free from the enemy's snares that would bring defeat into our lives. We will never know victory until we have been in a battle! Let us enter the battle we are assured of winning.

The adverse circumstances of our lives may well be the enemy seeking to destroy us and bring us to defeat, but we can turn the circumstances around by faith in Jesus. We can exercise our authority in Him, remove mountains of opposition and pummel problems that have their origin in the enemy's work. Alternatively, God at times works adverse circumstances into our lives to test our faith and trust in Him, while bringing to the surface the true condition of our hearts. This will enable Him to refine and cleanse in order for His healing and restoration to flow as we are conformed into His image. God is doing a deep work in our lives and will not allow us to remain spiritually immature.

God will enable us to realise our God-given dreams when we yield to His sovereign plan for our lives.

> *'There is a way that seems right to a man but the end it leads to death.'* (Proverbs 14:12)

We produce unnecessary stress when we fight against God insisting we know best. He is trying to bring in the very best, but we tend to settle only for the good.

The Father in His love and kindness desires our best at all times. He loves us, cares for us and has plans and purposes for our lives. The enemy is against us and will resist us at every turn. God wants us to rise up and take hold of all that He has secured for us on the cross, so that we may enter in and take possession of what is rightfully ours in Christ Jesus. Whether we do or not rests entirely with ourselves. The choice is ours!

The author can be contacted at:

Sovereign Ministries
Renewal Centre
Marton Street
Lancaster LA1 1XX
England

Tel: (0)1524 382141
Fax: (0)1524 382141
Email: sovmin@aol.com